On the Incarnation of Christ

On the Incarnation of Christ

Against the Heretic Nestorius

John Cassian, Abbot of Marseilles

Translated by
A Father of the Oxford Oratory

GRACEWING

First published in England in 2018
by
Gracewing
2 Southern Avenue
Leominster
Herefordshire HR6 0QF
United Kingdom
www.gracewing.co.uk

ISBN 978 085244 897 7

Typeset by Word and Page, Chester, UK

Cover design by Bernardita Peña Hurtado

CONTENTS

INTRODUCTION

THE LITTLE TREATISE ON THE INCARNATION is of a very different character from Cassian's better-known works, the *Institutes* and the *Collations*. They have always been famous as works of spirituality, familiar at least by reputation even during the dark days of the Jansenists, and they have received well-deserved attention in more recent decades. This third work, however, has never received much popular notice, and it must be admitted that were it not for the name of Cassian, it would probably be quite forgotten. After all, one might think, it deals with long-past controversies, the debate over the nature of Christ, which so occupied the Church during the fourth and fifth centuries, matters that were settled centuries ago.

Cassian wrote the *De Incarnatione* in 429, at the request of Leo, Archdeacon of Rome, as part of the build-up to the condemnation of Nestorius at the Synod of Rome in 430 and the general Council of Ephesus in 431. Leo himself, of course, was to become Pope in 440, and intervene conclusively in the next Christological crisis, the Monophysite over-reaction to Nestorianism, settled at the Council of Chalcedon in 451.

The great divisions which afflicted Christendom in the sixteenth century left the doctrine of the nature of Christ largely intact, so that Catholics, Orthodox and Protestants could at least agree on the conclusions of the first four General Councils (Nicea I, Constantinople I, Ephesus and Chalcedon). Only small fringe groups ventured to differ. That all changed in the twentieth century, when the 'modernist' or 'liberal' movement in theology gained control over most Protestant and many Catholic writers, and the old conclusions could no longer be taken for granted. Many moderns, who still claim to be Christians, have consciously or unconsciously revived all the erroneous opinions which Cassian nicely terms the 'weeds' in the garden of God (Book I, c. 2).

Perhaps the reason for this was the uncritical acceptance of the conclusions of the so-called 'higher critics', who investigated the texts of Scripture, purporting to treat them objectively and scientifically, in the same way that other scholars examined other examples of ancient literature. By the 1890s the view of Harnack had prevailed, that the real essence of Christianity, the core teaching of Jesus of Nazareth, was that the world was about to come to a catastrophic end, and that only his followers would survive to rule in the new Kingdom. It was accepted that all the 'early Christians' lived in the daily expectation of an imminent return of Jesus Christ (which came to be known as the 'Parousia'), and that they had, therefore, no interest in establishing any sort of organized Church, since there was not going to be time to get it going. (In other words, the motivation behind this extraordinary re-reading of Scripture was an antipathy to organized religion, in particular the Catholic Church.) What was very obvious was that if that really was the essential teaching of Jesus of Nazareth, he was absolutely wrong. The world was still very much in existence nineteen hundred years later. If he was as fundamentally wrong as that, then clearly he could not have any special divine knowledge. After a rather ludicrous attempt called 'kenotic theology', which maintained that Jesus really was the Son of God but had somehow forgotten the fact, most 'liberal' thinkers settled for the simple solution that he was no more than a good man, with some mistaken ideas, but who could be admired as a model for unselfish moral behaviour.

Among Protestant bodies, the liberal approach became more or less standard among 'educated' people, who allowed themselves free rein in challenging, and eventually contradicting, every established Christian position, disposing of doctrine in the first half of the twentieth century, and morals in the second. The reaction from the Evangelical wing, which actually represented the majority of Protestant believers, was to reject any sort of scientific or philosophical analysis, and cling to a simple version of the traditional faith, making it a virtue to believe without questioning.

The subtleties of Patristic thought were ignored, but the basic conclusion held, that Jesus really is God, and that we are obliged to obey the moral commandments found in Scripture. Only a few Protestant theologians of calibre, such as Eric Maskell and George Caird, dared to disagree with the 'established results of modern criticism' and argue that there was a respectable academic case for orthodox conclusions after all.

Catholics and Orthodox tended to ignore the 'higher critics' at first, until the 1960s when many Catholic theologians suddenly swallowed the entire liberal Protestant agenda, and rapidly moved to positions even more extreme. Becoming ever more shrill in their objections to any restraint on their ideas, offered by a Papacy concerned for the distress of ordinary Catholics, the new liberals arrogated to themselves an infallibility which they were certainly not prepared to concede to Jesus of Nazareth. As a result translations of both Scripture and liturgy were slanted towards the old Harnack view, and the impression given that it was not only the 'early Christians' who believed the world was about to end, but that modern Christians did so too. Liturgy was understood as a commemorative meal, in memory of a long-dead Jewish carpenter, but in the expectation that any minute now he would reappear, for the end of the world was now really imminent. Politicians in the 1980s did their best to bring it about.

They must have been seriously disappointed when the fateful year 2000 passed without incident. And as the liberals, both Protestant and Catholic, grow older and retire from their university posts, their place is being taken by radical young thinkers who are quite prepared to ask all the questions they can think of, just as St Thomas Aquinas and his contemporaries did, and are not ashamed to come to the sound old orthodox conclusions, so that the term 'radical orthodoxy' has come to be the label of some of the most dynamic writers of today.

Now how can Cassian be relevant to this twenty-first century situation? The treatise we present here is a refutation of the heresy we know as Nestorianism, but in the process deals effectively with many other erroneous ideas on the nature of Christ. Cassian refers often to the older errors, those of Ebion, who considered Jesus was a mere man, and Carinthus, who thought He was true God but only pretending to be human; of Marcion who denied that the dreadful God of the Old Testament was in any way related to the kindly Father of Jesus Christ (he had to cut out a very large proportion of the New Testament to maintain this), and Sabellius, who thought that 'Father, Son and Holy Spirit' were alternative names for the same person. More recently, he mentions the Arians, who began by maintaining that Jesus was a super-human being, higher than all the angels, though not really God. In Cassian's time many northern nations admitted to being Arians, but probably simplified the teaching, taking Jesus as a mere man, through whom God spoke. That seems also to have been the position of Pelagius, who is specifically attacked in the fifth book of the treatise. Pelagius, of course, is best remembered as claiming that it is open to anyone to reform their lives and make themselves perfect, just as the man Jesus of Nazareth made himself so perfect that he was found worthy to become God. (Cassian mentions that Pelagius came from the 'City of the Belgae' (Book I, cap 2), which has puzzled later scribes and editors. Is it possible that he means *Venta Belgarum*, in other words Winchester?)

Nestorius, Patriarch of Constantinople, became famous when he publicly denied that it was appropriate to call the Virgin Mary *Theotokos*, the one who brought God to birth, or simply 'Mother of God'. He denied this, not through any wish to defame Mary, but because he thought she could only be the mother of the human being, Jesus of Nazareth, not of the eternal Word of God. He agreed to call her *Christotokos*, 'Mother of Christ', but could not accept that her Son was truly God at the time of his birth. Indeed he calls Jesus the *Theodochos*, the 'God-receiver', an assumed man who accepted Godhead into himself. Although Nestorius himself probably never drew the logical conclusions that others found in his first premises, the inevitable result was that people considered Jesus a mere man, one who through his own efforts became worthy to receive godhead at some stage of his career, but who was not essentially the same person as the Word of God.

Now all these ancient heresies, Ebionism, Cerinthianism, Marcionism, Sabellianism, Arianism, Pelagianism and Nestorianism, can be found happily ensconced in the common rooms of our great universities. In a more popular version, the idea that Jesus could receive godhead as a result of his moral and spiritual efforts, leads to the realization that everyone can receive the godhead, or allow the godhead to express herself within them, so that religion becomes a matter of spiritualised self-expression, free from the external trammels of organized doctrine. In the 1980s a small book circulated widely among Catholic teachers in England which assured them that 'Jesus had no hot line to God', and that everyone has equal access to the 'godself', so that religious instruction is simply a matter of helping each pupil to discover the divinity within them, to model their belief and practice on what they find there. Jesus is God only in the sense that all of us are.

Cassian replies to Nestorius in a long diatribe, often addressing him directly, and in no uncertain terms. Your heresy, he tells him, is not new, it is simply a re-hash of the previous ones, and in particular of Pelagianism. In book five he shows us how similar the ideas are: both Pelagius and Nestorius effectively treat Jesus as a mere man, and give the impression that anyone can win their way to heaven as Jesus did. Incidentally, this shows how far from the truth it is to accuse Cassian of any compromise with Pelagianism. As we have shown in the introduction to our translation of the *Collations* (Gracewing, 2015), the Jansenist attack on Cassian, accusing him of being a 'Semi-Pelagian', was motivated really by the fact that Cassian would have no truck with the loathsome doctrine of predestination to eternal damnation, the denial of any human co-operation with the grace of God. Cassian, like the Catholic Church, teaches that grace is a free and unmerited gift of God, by which he invites us to share in his life, but we have the free will to accept or reject that grace.

Most of the treatise is based on Scriptural texts, because Cassian can take it for granted that everyone who reads him will accept that Scripture is definitive, and that an appropriate text from Scripture can settle an argument. In doing this he is no 'fundamentalist': he insists that a text must be taken complete and in context, and that an understanding of literary forms is necessary to interpret the text. For instance he aptly points out the use of the figure of speech called *synecdoche* (Book VI, cap. 23). Here, we must admit, he will be of little use against our moderns, who have no such respect for the inerrancy of Scripture. We can only point out that Cassian has demonstrated the beliefs of the Biblical authors, in particular what the New Testament writers held. Even those who will not accept that the scriptures are inspired, must admit that they are a record of the beliefs of the first Christians. Cassian shows us that the developed doctrine of the fifth century is an authentic reflection of the beliefs of the first. The popular fantasy that in the beginning Christianity was very, very simple, and it was only the fourth and fifth-century theologians who complicated it by inventing doctrine, can be refuted from Cassian's use of Scriptural texts.

In Book VI he turns to the Creed, commenting aptly that he would not use it in argument against an Arian, who did not accept that formula, but could use it when speaking to one who had grown up in a church where the Creed was the standard of faith. An Arian, he implies, can be forgiven for being loyal to the faith in which he was brought up—by this time Arianism was well established as a denomination—but one who was brought up as a Catholic really ought to be loyal to the creed of his own baptism. Catholic controversialists have always taken this line, to be understanding and sympathetic to those brought up in error from childhood, but severe on those who have once known the truth and have wandered away from it. Cassian does not quote the familiar Niceno-Constantinopolitan Creed, but the slightly different Creed of the Church of Antioch, for the simple reason that Nestorius was born there. In citing the Creed, he makes the point that God speaks through the bishops of our own day just as he did through the prophets and apostles who wrote the Bible. The Word of God is expressed through the words of men in both Scripture and Conciliar decree. In effect, Cassian teaches the fundamental Catholic principle of ongoing revelation through both Scripture and Tradition, and the authority of the living Church.

In the last Book, Cassian meets some of Nestorius' problems head on. If Nestorius cannot believe in the incarnation on the grounds that it is contrary to natural law, then he is in fact limiting the power of God to suspend his own decrees. Nature herself is already full of paradox, as we can see in the familiar example of the hatching of basilisk eggs (Book VII, cap. 5). Nestorius' misuse of Scripture is exposed, and Cassian shows how the true interpretation of the Bible leads only to a Catholic conclusion. In the same way he quotes the Fathers, the great writers who have been accepted as authoritative by Orthodox and Catholic alike, although in this case he is talking about his own contemporaries. Athanasius and Gregory were long dead, but Jerome had only very recently died, and Augustine was still alive; despite their differences they were obviously accepted as reliable guides in theology. Most favoured of all was St John Chrysostom, the greatest of the bishops of Constantinople, who had also only died recently, a close friend and mentor of Cassian, who had indeed been ordained by him. Nestorius, his successor, is appropriately silenced with reference to the great confessor of the faith, and Cassian ends with a ringing appeal to the people of Constantinople to stand firm in their faith.

Those who have read Chrysostom will not be so sanguine about the good sense of the people of the Great City, but in this case Cassian's hopes were realized. After the Council of Ephesus the Nestorian faction lost influence within the Empire, and survived only outside the borders in the wilderness. Nevertheless it was in that wilderness that Nestorianism lived on to become one of the formative influences on Islam. If Jesus is a mere man, through whom the Word of God spoke, then he is really no more than one of a series of prophets, and although he can be recognized as the promised Messiah, and his birth of a Virgin confidently asserted, he need not be the last of the prophets. The doctrine of the Trinity is unnecessary once we have agreed that Jesus is not really God, and the door is open to the simple affirmation of the oneness of God revealed through his servant the Prophet. Catholicism found its definitive formulation in the teaching of the Councils of Ephesus and Chalcedon, that Jesus Christ is true God and true Man, but if we deny that, then there is no logical reason for rejecting the claims of the other dominant world religion.

The text we have translated is that edited by Michael Petschenig, in the Corpus Scriptorum Ecclesiasticorum Latinorum (vol. XVII), published in Vienna in 1888 (and reprinted in 2004), but with reference also to the more accessible Patrologia Latina (vol. 50, 1–272). Passages in the Patrologia omitted in CSEL are given in square brackets. Biblical quotations are taken from the Douai version, because that is a literal translation of the Latin Vulgate which Cassian used.

John Cassian, Abbot of Marseilles

ON THE INCARNATION OF CHRIST

AGAINST THE HERETIC NESTORIUS

Preface

To Leo, Bishop of the City of Rome

WHEN I HAD FINISHED the books of spiritual Conferences, which are more distinguished for their content than their style, since my inexpert words are no match for the high teaching of those holy men, I had intended, and all but resolved, to anchor myself in the harbour of silence, after exposing my shameful ignorance in that way. Thus I might have been able to atone for my audacious garrulity by respectful reserve. But, O my revered Leo, you have overcome my set intention, in your worthy zeal and commanding affection. My love for the Roman Church and respect for the sacred hierarchy have taken me up and brought me out of that silent retreat I intended, onto the stage of the public forum. I am still blushing for my earlier work, and you are forcing me to begin a new one. I was unequal to the lesser task, and you are making me face up to a greater. Even in those other writings which my poor wit had offered as a sacrifice to Our Lord I never tried to compile anything or compose it without the authority of a bishop: indeed, the dignity of my words and style is enhanced by you. Formerly we were bidden to write about the teaching of Our Lord, but now you are requesting me to say something of his very incarnation and his majesty. Earlier we were led into the sanctuary of the Temple at the hands of the priest, now with your guidance and support we are entering the Holy of Holies. It is a great honour, but a perilous path, since one may not reach the inner sanctuary and grasp the palm of God's reward before overcoming our enemies.

Your request, or rather your command, is to raise my weak fists against the recently arisen heresy, the new enemy of the faith, to stand with my mouth open against the pestilential breath of the vile serpent, in other words that, with me as your snake-charmer, the strength of prophecy and the power of God's word might burst asunder the dragon which has risen up with his encircling coils against the Church of God. I will bow to your command and obey your will, for I have more confidence in you than in myself, especially since it is the love of Jesus Christ my Lord that has moved you and commanded you to do this. But you must entreat him, by whom you have given me this order, to bring my ordained task into effect. It is your concern rather than mine that is at stake, your judgment more at risk than my own. For myself, whether I be equal to carry out your orders or no, I have an excuse in following obedience and humility, and there is more virtue in my compliance than in my abilities. It is easy to give full satisfaction by obeying, for the real task, the wonder, is to have the intention even where the strength is lacking. The business is yours, yours the concern, yours the risk: pray and beseech, therefore, that my clumsiness does not prejudice your decision. If we prove unequal to your project, however easily I may obtain indulgence through my obedience, you will still appear to have made a bad decision and chosen the wrong person to command.

❖

✟ BOOK ONE ✟

I. The myths of poetry tell us that when you cut off the heads of the hydra, more numerous ones grow out of its own wounds, so that, incredibly, the monster gains from its losses, the more often it is put to death. Whatever the cutting sword strikes off is doubled by its astounding resilience, until the worthy hero, after labouring away at the task he has undertaken, and seeing his efforts rendered so often vain, reinforces his warlike strength with cunning. As they tell us, torches are brought, and as he cuts the many growths off the monster's body with his vorpal blade, he cauterises the wounds at once. Once he has seared the veins which were sprouting with such evil effect, he puts an end to the rebirth of the fiend.

In the same way, in the Church, heresy bears a resemblance to the hydra which the poets describe. Heresies also hiss against us with savage tongues; heresies also spit out lethal poison; heresies also are reborn from their severed heads. As the disease recurs, the healing must not cease, and the greater the sickness the more urgent becomes the cure. Our Lord and God is powerful enough, so that what pagan myth tells of the death of the hydra is true of the wars of the Church. The burning blade of the Holy Spirit cauterises the wounds of that evil fecundity to prevent new heresies from growing, until the veins are exhausted and that dreadful growth ceases at last.

II. This monstrous offspring is nothing new in the Church, and the harvest of the Lord's field has always had to tolerate burrs and brambles, and the persistent contamination of clinging tares. Hence we had Ebionites, Sabellians, Arians, later Eunomians and Macedonians, then Photinians and Apollinarians and the other weeds of the Church; thorns multiply and choke the fruits of true faith. Ebion was the first, who so emphasised the Lord's incarnation that he stripped him of his divine nature. In reaction to that, there broke out the heresy of Sabellius, who maintained that there is no distinction between Father, Son and Holy Spirit, and did all he could to mix up the Holy and ineffable Trinity in a blasphemous confusion. After that there followed the perverse wickedness of Arius, who avoided confusing the sacred Persons by saying that in the Trinity there were different and distinct natures. After that came Eunomius, equally perverse, who admitted that each person of the Trinity is similarly divine, but maintained that they differ in rank from each other, admitting their similarity but denying their equality. Macedonius, on the other hand, blasphemed intolerably against the Holy Spirit by admitting that the Father and the Son are of one substance, but calling the Holy Spirit a creature. Thus he impugned the whole Godhead, for you cannot strike at one person of the Trinity without disbelieving in the whole. Photinus admitted that Jesus who was born of the Virgin is God, but was mistaken in imagining that he began to be God at the same time that he began to be man. Apollinaris was so careless in describing the union of manhood and Godhead that he imagined Our Lord had no human soul, for it is no less mistaken to add the wrong attributes to Our Lord Jesus Christ as it is to deny them. If anything is said about him that is not true, it is an error even if it appears to be an honour.

Thus each one in the same way produced one heresy from another, each differing from the other, but all opposed to the one faith. Now in our own time we have watched a poisonous heresy arise, especially in the city of the Belgae [Winchester ?]; an error, certainly, but of uncertain name. Since it has recently sprung from the ancient stock of the Ebionites, it is unclear whether it should be called an ancient heresy or a novel one. It is newly asserted, but old in error. It asserts, blasphemously, that Our Lord Jesus Christ was born a mere man, and that he afterwards attained the honour and power of God through his human merits, not through his divine nature. Thus he did not always possess divinity through the property of the godhead united to himself, but earned it afterwards as a reward for his labours and his passion. The affirmation that Our Lord and Saviour was not God when he was born, but was assumed by God, is cognate to this present heresy, closely related to it indeed; it was held both by the Ebionites and our new heretics, lying between them in time and linking them both in perversity. There are a number of points of similarity other than the one I have mentioned, but it would take a long time to recount them all. Our present task is not to describe the errors of the past, but to refute those of the present day.

III. There is one point which I think should not be passed over, which is specific to the heresy I have mentioned and derived from the Pelagian errors: if they say that Jesus Christ was a mere man, and that he lived without any stain of sin, it follows that they must assert that any man who wishes can be free from sin. If the mere man Jesus Christ could be sinless, without God's help, it seems logical that any man should be able to achieve as much as that mere man did, without fellowship with God. It is tantamount to denial that there be any difference between Our Lord Jesus Christ and any other man, to claim that anyone were able to achieve, by his own effort and industry, what Christ merited by his zeal and labours. It results in the even greater lunacy of saying that Our

Lord Jesus Christ came into this world, not to redeem the human race, but to give us an example of good deeds. Thus any man who followed his teaching should be able to walk in the same path of virtue and earn the same reward for that virtue. In this way they did their best to deny all value to the gift of Christ's coming, and the grace of divine redemption, claiming that all men can, by their way of life, attain the same reward that God granted to him who died for our salvation. They go on to say that our Lord and Saviour only became Christ after his baptism, and God only after his resurrection, attributing one title to the sacrament of his anointing, the other to the merits of his passion. Thus you can see that our new heretic [Nestorius], whose heresy is far from new, in claiming that Our Lord and Saviour was born a mere man, is saying exactly the same thing as the Pelagians before him. The blasphemous consequence of that error is that, if Jesus Christ as a mere man was able to live without sin, then any man likewise can be without sin. Our Lord's work of redemption thus becomes unnecessary, as Pelagius said, if men can attain the kingdom of heaven by their own efforts. The outcome shows us clearly how true this is. It happened that our new heretic did support the Pelagian cause by his influence, and in his writings defended their conclusions. He was their patron in secret, or rather by deceit, and his wicked sympathies lay with the wickedness that was akin to his own, for he recognized the same spirit and intention in them. He was thus grieved that their heresy was detected and removed from the Church, for he knew that it was equally perverse and linked with his own.

IV. Nevertheless some who originated in that pestilential and prickly stock were in the event saved by the help of God and by prayer; we should pray then to the Lord our God that those who have followed that earlier heresy, or this new one, and have made a similarly bad beginning may come to a similarly good outcome. Leporius, for example, was first a monk and then a priest, who had been trained, or rather we should say corrupted, by Pelagius, and went into Gaul as one of the first and most important preachers of the said heresy. He was admonished by us, and brought by God to repudiate his ill-considered beliefs magnificently. His conversion is as wonderful as the uncorrupted faith of the rest of our people; to renounce error soundly is second only to having refrained from entering into it. When he had come to his senses he confessed his error with tears, but without embarrassment, in Africa where he was then and still is now; moreover he wrote letters to every city in Gaul, confessing with grief and tears, so that in the places where his deviation had first been heard, there might his conversion be known; those who had been witnesses to his error might also witness his correction of it.

V. I think I ought to insert a few extracts from the confession of Leporius, or rather his retractation, for two reasons, to produce evidence of his emendation, and to give an example to those who are wavering. Those who were not ashamed to follow him in error need not blush to follow him in its correction. Those who suffer from a similar illness may be cured by a similar remedy. Once Leporius had acknowledged the perversity of his opinions, and seen the light of faith, he wrote to the bishops of Gaul, beginning thus: 'Reverend lords and most beatific high priests, I know not where to begin in accusing myself, I find nothing in me to defend. I was so ignorant and proud, so foolishly open to evil suggestion, so intemperate in my zeal, so feeble and faint my faith, to tell the truth, that all those things combined in me to the extent that I was reduced to shame; now I am both amazed and gratified that I have come to proper obedience, and that these ideas were able to be removed from my soul.' A little further on he added, 'We were so far from appreciating the power of God, being wise in our own estimation, that we imagined God acted through lesser agents, so that we said that a man was born along with God, and we attributed divine actions to God alone, and thought all his human actions belonged to the man alone—in effect we were introducing a fourth person to the Holy Trinity, and were on the way to making not one but two Christs out of the one Son of God; and may Christ who is himself our Lord and our God preserve us from that! We confess, therefore, that Jesus Christ, Our Lord and our God, is the one Son of God, born to himself, of the Father before the ages, and made man for us in time through the Holy Spirit, and Mary, ever a virgin; he is God born for us. We confess also the two natures of the flesh and of the Word, and we acknowledge with loving faith that he is one and the same, God and man, inseparable for ever. From the moment that he took flesh, we proclaim that every attribute of God passed into his humanity, and everything that was human came into the Godhead. In this way do we understand that the Word was made Flesh, not that he began to be in any way what he was not before through any conversion or change, but that by the power of God's providence the Word of the Father was pleased to become a real man, without ever leaving the Father; the Only-begotten was made flesh by a mysterious process which he alone knows, for it is ours to believe, his to understand. In this way God the Word is man by assuming all that is human; and the assumed humanity, by receiving all that is of God, can be none other than God. We do not say that his nature is in any way diminished because he is said to be incarnate and of combined nature, for God knows how to combine the natures without any corruption, although it is a true combination of nature; he knows too how to accept things into himself without growth, just as he can give himself totally without suffering any loss. We do not restrict ourselves to our own level of intelligence and imagine we can follow the analogy of visible and experiential evidence on what happens when created things that are equal enter into each other, so that God and man would be mixed together, making some sort of third substance by mingling the Flesh and the Word. Far be it from us to believe that the two natures were somehow reduced and conflated into one substance, for a mixture of that sort would be detrimental to both natures. For God contains, but is not contained, penetrates but is not penetrated, fills but is not filled; he is wholly and at once everywhere, and is extended everywhere; it was by the outpouring of his power that, in his love for us, he was combined with human nature.'

A little further on he writes, 'He was therefore truly born for us of the Holy Spirit and of Mary ever a virgin, God and Man, Jesus Christ, the Son of God. As the Word and the Flesh were one, in each other, each substance remaining in its natural perfection, without any diminution, the attributes of divinity were communicated to the humanity, those of humanity to the divinity. There was not one person who was God and another who was man, but one and the same person, God who is man, and correspondingly man who is called and really is God, Jesus Christ, the only Son of God. It is therefore our belief and our duty to acknowledge that Our Lord Jesus Christ, the Son of God, true God, whom we confess to have been with the Father always, and equal to the Father before time began, was the same person who took flesh within time and is God made man. We do not believe that he advanced towards God by degrees over a period of time, nor that his status before the resurrection was other than that after the resurrection, but that he possessed always the same fullness and power.'

Further on, he continues, 'Because God the Word descended into humanity by worthily assuming manhood into himself, and man ascended to be the Word through being assumed by God, God the Word was wholly made whole man. Not that God the Father was made man, nor the Holy Spirit, but the Only-begotten of the Father; thus flesh and Word together are accepted as one person, and so we believe faithfully and without doubt that the one same Son of God, in two inseparable natures, was called a giant in the days of his flesh (Psalm 18:6), and truly did all that is human, while truly possessing all that is of God. "For although he was crucified in weakness, yet he liveth by the power of God"' (II Corinthians 13:4).

VI. This, then, was the confession of Leporius, which is the faith of all Catholics; it was approved both by the bishops of Africa, where he was writing, and the bishops of Gaul to whom he wrote. Nor is there anyone who could be displeased by this profession of faith, without incurring the charge of unbelief, for to deny defined belief is an admission of bad faith. The common consent ought

to be enough to refute all heresy, since the authority of the whole
world is a clear indication of truth, and when no one disagrees
there is perfect certainty. Hence if anyone wants to oppose this
teaching, there is a clear case for refusing to hear his opinions, to
condemn indeed his perversity. One who attacks the consensus of
the world makes his own condemnation known in advance, and he
who denies what all have agreed will find no audience. Once the
truth has been agreed by everyone, anything contrary to that truth
can be recognized as false by the very fact that it dissents from
the truth. That fact alone is sufficient to condemn it for dissenting
from the agreed truth. Nevertheless a reasoned argument is no
obstacle to true reason, and truth is more brilliant the more it is
expounded, it is better for those in error to be corrected by a saving
explanation than simply to be severely condemned. The ancient
heresy in our new heretics must be cured by us, in so far as we are
able with God's help, so that they may receive healing in divine
mercy, and their cure may give a witness to our holy faith greater
than any example of severity which could be furnished by their
condemnation. May Truth himself be present in our discussions
and arguments about himself; may it bring healing to human error
through that love by which God was pleased to visit men, for the
principal reason why he wished to be born among men on earth
was so that no further place might remain for error.

❖

✠ BOOK TWO ✠

I. In the previous book I promised to demonstrate how Nestorius, our new heretic, springs up from the stock of ancient heresies, so that the rightful condemnation of the earlier heretics might be sufficient to bring a just sentence of condemnation on him. Since they have the same roots, and grow from the same furrows, he is adequately refuted by the condemnation of his models, especially when the opinions they proffered were well refuted by his immediate predecessors, whom he failed to imitate well. Hence one or other of these parties, those who were condemned or those who stood corrected, should have provided Nestorius with enough of an example. Those capable of receiving correction provide healing through their very correction; those who are incorrigible can teach by their own condemnation. Nevertheless, I do not want to be thought to be prejudging them rather than assessing them fairly, so I will set out their pestilential proposition, or rather their blasphemous insanity, 'in all things taking the shield of faith, ... and the sword of the spirit (which is the word of God)' (Ephesians 6:16–17). In this way the sword of God's word which once cut off the head of the ancient serpent may once again strike off the head of the resurgent dragon now in its present coils. Since the error of Nestorius is the same as was theirs of old, what cut off the one will serve to amputate the other. The reborn serpents are blasting the Church of the Lord with their pestilential breath, and making many faint with their hissing, the cure which worked against the old wounds must be applied anew to our present ills. Thus even if that former action be insufficient to cure the disease, our present work may operate to heal those who are weak.

II. So, heretic, whoever you be, you deny that God was born of the Virgin, and that Mary, the mother of Our Lord Jesus Christ may be called *Theotokos*, meaning the mother of God, but you call her *Christotokos*, the mother merely of the Christ, not of God. You assert that 'no one can be parent of one older than herself'. This is a stupid argument, if you think you can understand the birth of God in a carnal sense, and comprehend the mystery of majesty within human reasoning: we shall deal with this point later if God permit. But now let us demonstrate that Christ is God and Mary is the Mother of God, from the word of God. Here is the angel of God speaking to the shepherds about the birth of God: 'For this day is born to you a Saviour, who is Christ the Lord, in the city of David' (Luke 2:11). Lest you think this refers only to Christ as man, he adds the names of Lord and Saviour, so that if you acknowledge him to be Saviour, you cannot doubt that he is God. Since the power to save belongs to God alone, you can be sure that he has the power of God, once you have learnt that the power to save is in him. But maybe this stretches your powers of belief, because the angel named the Lord as Saviour rather than as God or Son of God? Can you be so impious as to deny that he is God when you have acknowledged him as Saviour? Hear, then, the archangel Gabriel announcing to Mary the Virgin, 'The Holy Ghost shall come upon thee, and the power of the Most High shall overshadow thee. And therefore also the Holy that shall be born of thee shall be called the Son of God' (Luke 1:35). Do you see how he tells us about the work of God as a way of leading up to the news that God is to be born? 'The Holy Ghost shall come upon thee, and the power of the Most High shall overshadow thee.' How beautifully speaks the angel, explaining the majestic work of God by his divine words! It was the Holy Spirit that sanctified the Virgin's womb, breathing within her the power of his divinity, and instilling himself into human nature. What was foreign to himself he made his own, taking it up into his own power and majesty. Lest human weakness be incapable of receiving the advent of the divine, the Virgin whom we all revere was strengthened by the power of the Most High; he spread the protection of his shadow over her to give strength to her human frailty, so that weak human nature did not fail to complete the wonderful mystery of that holy conception, being sustained by the overshadowing divinity.

'The Holy Ghost', he said, 'shall come upon thee, and the power of the Most High shall overshadow thee.' If the man that was to be born of the pure Virgin was to be no more than a mere man, what need was there for such an annunciation of his holy coming? Why so great a working of divine power? If only a man was to be born of man, only flesh from flesh, a simple command, the bare will of God, would have been enough. If the simple will of God and his command was enough to form the heavens and to found the earth, to create the sea, and moreover to create thrones and dominations, angels and archangels, principalities and powers, the whole host of heaven, and the thousand thousand countless armies of God—for it is said, 'he spoke and they were made: he commanded and they were created' (Psalm 32/3:9)—why was it insufficient for the conception of a single man (as you claim he is), that word which was enough to create everything that is of God? Could the power and majesty of God be unequal to causing the birth of one little child, when it had sufficed for the establishment of all things on earth and in heaven? All those works came to pass through the mere command of God, but the nativity only in his presence, for God could not be conceived of man except as his own gift, could not be born except by his own descent. Therefore the archangel announced to the Virgin the sacred majesty that was to come, for since so great a matter could not be brought to pass by human effort, his dignity might be discerned in his conception, as it was to be in his birth. The Word, the Son, descended; the splendour of the Holy Spirit was present, the power of the Father overshadowed, so that the whole Trinity co-operated in the mystery of that holy conception. 'Therefore also' did he say, 'the Holy that shall be born of thee shall be called the Son of God.' The word 'therefore' was needed, to show how once those things had happened, the next things would follow, because God had been present in the conception, he would be God also in his birth. The maiden did not understand how this could be, but he explained it in the words, 'The Holy Ghost shall come upon thee, and the power of the Most High shall overshadow thee. And therefore also the Holy that shall be born of thee shall be called the Son of God.' This is as much as to say, 'you should know what a great thing is being done, and what a great mystery is unfolding, for the whole majesty of God is coming into you, and the Son of God will be born of you.'

Is there any ambiguity in this? What more could be said? He said that God would be present, that the Son of God would be born. Tell me, now, if you please, how could the Son of God not be himself God? Or how could she who gave birth to God not be *Theotokos*, the Mother of God? These words alone should be enough for you—indeed they are great and truly sufficient.

III. Now since the evidence for that holy nativity is so abundant, and since all that was written in scripture was intended to be a witness to that nativity, let us briefly examine some parts of the Old Testament that speak of the annunciation of God. Thus you may understand that the birth of God which would be of a Virgin was not only announced when it was about to happen, but was predicted from the very beginning of the world. In that way, when the indescribable work came to be done, the fact that future events had always been predicted might make it easier to believe when it happened.

The prophet Isaiah, then, said, 'Behold, a virgin shall conceive and bear a son: and his name shall be called Emmanuel, which, being interpreted, is God with us' (Isaiah 7:14, Matthew 1:23). What room is there for ambiguity or doubt? The prophet said that a virgin would conceive, and a virgin has conceived. He said a child would be born, and a child has been born. He said he would be called God, and he is called God. He is called by the name that belongs to his nature. Now since the Spirit of God has said we should call him God, anyone who makes himself a stranger to the agreed title of divinity proves himself to be destitute of the Spirit of God. 'Behold, a virgin shall conceive,' he says, 'and bear a son: and his name shall be called Emmanuel, which, being interpreted, is God with us.' But maybe the unbeliever will excuse himself by claiming that when the prophet says he should be called God, it refers merely to the name, not to the splendour of divinity. But how then do we explain that in the Gospels Christ is never called by that name, for we cannot say that the Spirit of God spoke through the prophet untruthfully? We can only conclude that the prophesy foretold the title of his divinity, not his earthly name. The Man who is one person with God received another name in the Gospels, so that the latter name must be the one relating to his humanity, the former to his divinity.

Let us continue and cite some more truthful texts to prove the truth, for in talking about God, his divinity is established best of all in his own words. The same prophet Isaiah said in another place, 'A child is born to us, and a son is given to us, and the government is upon his shoulder: and his name shall be called, Angel of great Counsel, God the Mighty, the Father of the world to come, the Prince of Peace' (Isaiah 9:6). Just as the prophet earlier said he would be called Emmanuel, now here he says he will be called 'Angel of great Counsel, God the Mighty, the Father of the world to come, the Prince of Peace', but nowhere in the Gospels do we read that he was called by those names. Thus we may understand that these are not earthly names, but divine: the name he received in the Gospels was a human name, the others belong to his unbegotten dignity. Since he was God, to be born among men, so his names were distinguished by divine providence, so that he could bear a human name in the flesh, and the names of God in his divinity. 'Angel of great Counsel', they will call him, and 'God the Mighty, the Father of the world to come, the Prince of Peace.' This does not mean, O heretics all, whoever you be, this does not mean that the prophet, when filled with the spirit of God, compared the one who was to be born to a cast statue, or a poetic metaphor, as you seem to assert! 'For a child is born to us, and a son is given to us, and the government is upon his shoulder: and his name shall be called, Angel of great Counsel, God the Mighty ...' Do not imagine that the one he announced as God was other than the one who was born in the flesh, for he specifies his birth, saying, 'a child is born to us, and a son is given to us.' See how many titles the prophet uses to show that he was really born in the flesh! He says he was born, that he was little, specifying that he was a little child, so that he could stress that there was an offspring born. The Spirit of God assuredly foresaw the blasphemous perversity of our heretics, and used titles of true significance to show the world that it was God who was to be born. Thus if heretics want to blaspheme, they can find no justification for doing so. 'A child is born to us, and a son is given to us, and the government is upon his shoulder: and his name shall be called, Angel of great Counsel, God the Mighty, the Father of the world to come, the Prince of Peace.' This little child who is to be born is called prince of peace, and father of the world to come, and God the mighty. What room is there for disagreement? There is no possibility of separating the little one who is born from the God who is born in him, for the one whom he says will be born is called the father of the world to come; the little one that he announces is named God the mighty. What have you to say in your defence, O heretic? Everything is sealed and settled, there is no way for you to escape. The error which you do not acknowledge willingly you must now be forced to admit!

We are not content with those texts: let us investigate what else the Holy Spirit has said through another prophet. 'Shall a man afflict God? For you afflict me' (Malachi 3:8). So that the words of the prophet might be made more evident, he prophesies, speaking in the person of the one he foretells, about the passion of Our Lord. 'Shall a man afflict God? For you afflict me.' Surely these words must apply to our Lord and God when he was led to his crucifixion! Why, then, do you not acknowledge me as your Redeemer? Why are you ignorant that God put on flesh for you? You have prepared a death for your Saviour, and led the author of your life away to death. I am your God, whom you have hung up; your God whom you have crucified. How can you be so wildly mistaken? 'Shall a man afflict God? For you afflict me.' Can you see how these words are spoken in reference to what actually happened? Do you want something more obvious, more evident? Can you see how the sacred texts apply to Our Lord Jesus Christ, born in the flesh, from his cradle even to the cross he bore? In one place you read that God was born in the flesh; in another you see God fastened to the cross. It was the prophets who spoke of God being born, and also of God being crucified, here most clearly. Thus the taking on of flesh could not be imagined to be detrimental to his divine honour, his lowly humanity and the shame of the passion could not infringe his majestic dignity. The humble meekness of his birth, and the loving mercy of his suffering should increase our love and reverence for him, for it would be the greatest scandal if we were to give him lesser honour after he has shown us so great a love.

IV. These texts can never be fully explained, for as his mercy towards us is so immense, it can never be completely comprehended; but let us pass on to look at St Paul the Apostle, that strong and evident witness to Christ. God spoke always through his heart,

so that he can tell us faithfully everything about God. This is how
he speaks of the grace and coming of Our Lord and God, he who
was sent as the chosen teacher of the gentiles to destroy gentile
superstition, 'The grace of God our Saviour hath appeared to all
men; instructing us, that, denying ungodliness and worldly desires,
we should live soberly and justly and godly in this world, looking
for the blessed hope and coming of the glory of the great God
and our Saviour Jesus Christ' (Titus 2:11–13). He says, 'the grace
of God our Saviour hath appeared to all men.' He chooses his
words well to show how that appearance indicated a new advent
of grace in his being born. This new gift of grace began to appear
from the moment God was made manifest, born into this world.
He shows us the light of the new grace in appropriate words, as
if pointing him out to us. What is demonstrated by the sudden
shining of a light may be rightly said to be manifest. Thus in the
Gospels we read that a star appeared to the wise men of the east,
and in Exodus it says, that an angel appeared to Moses in a flame
of fire in a bush (Exodus 3:2). In all sacred visions of this sort,
Scripture prefers to use these words, saying that he 'appeared',
meaning that the vision shone with an unwonted clarity. St Paul
also, describing the coming of heavenly grace which appeared at
that holy nativity, used words like 'appeared' to express shining,
saying that he appeared, meaning that he shone with the splendour
of a new light. 'The grace of God our Saviour hath appeared'—can
you pretend that this is in any way ambiguous, as if Christ was one
person and God another? Can you separate the Saviour from his
majestic name, the Lord from his divinity? See, this vessel of God
is speaking for God, and gives witness by his clear expression that
the grace of God appeared from Mary. Lest you should be able
to claim that God did not appear from Mary, he adds at once the
title Saviour, so that you must believe that he who was born of
Mary is God, for you cannot deny that he is Saviour, as the Gospel
says, 'this day is born to you a Saviour' (Luke 2:11).

What an admirable teacher has God granted to the gentiles!
He foresaw the coming of this heretical perversity in the future,
which would twist the language of God into dispute, and be

unashamed to slander God with his own titles. So that the heretic would not be able to separate the title of Saviour from his divinity, he placed the title God first; thus the name of God coming first would prove all the titles that followed. No one thereafter could imagine that Christ was a mere man, since he had taught us that he was God in the words that came before. For St Paul said, that we are 'looking for the blessed hope and coming of the glory of the great God and our Saviour Jesus Christ' (Titus 2:13). That teacher of divine wisdom realized that his simple doctrine would not be enough to frustrate the insidious subtlety of the devil's arguments, so he fortified the holy faith he was preaching with strong precautions. Since he had stated the names of God and Saviour before, he now adds the name Jesus Christ, in case you think the bare name of Saviour is not enough to indicate Our Lord Jesus Christ, and do not accept that it is the same Jesus Christ who is God, as the one you have recognized as Saviour and God. For what does he say? We are 'looking for the blessed hope and coming of the glory of the great God and our Saviour Jesus Christ.' None of the titles of Our Lord are lacking here—see him as God, as Saviour, as Jesus and as Christ. In seeing all these, you see them existing in God. You have heard him called God, and also Saviour; you have heard him called God and also Jesus; you have heard him called God and also Christ. What God has put together into one, may not be put asunder by the variety of titles. Whatever you are looking for you will find in the same person: the Saviour is God, Jesus is God, Christ is God. All the many titles you hear refer to the same authority. Since we know that the Saviour is God, Jesus is God, and Christ is God, it is open to our understanding to distinguish each of these titles but to unite them in one majesty. You have heard plainly that the One God is named in each case, so you may easily understand that the One God is in all. There is no room for you to claim from the variety of titles of Our Lord that there is a distinction of power, and to imagine a variety of persons because they are called by different names. You may not say, Christ was born of Mary, but God was not, for the Apostle proclaims him to be God. You may not say, Jesus was born of Mary, but God was not, for the Apostle bears witness that he is God. You may not say, the Saviour was born, but God was not, for the Apostle confirms that he is God. You have no escape: if you accept any of the titles of Our Lord, you must know that it is God you are naming. You have no argument, no evidence, no excuse to offer. You may refuse to believe with a wicked lack of faith, but you have no excuse to deny the truth.

V. Although we have begun to talk about the divine grace of Our Saviour and Lord, I would like to add more texts of Holy Scripture on this matter. We find in the Acts of the Apostles that the apostle James did not consider it at all right for those who had received the Gospel to be burdened with the yoke of the Old Law: he argues thus, 'Why tempt you God to put a yoke upon the necks of the disciples which neither our fathers nor we have been able to bear? But, by the grace of the Lord Jesus Christ, we believe to be saved, in like manner as they also' (Acts 15:10–11). The apostle tells us clearly that the gift of grace was given through Jesus Christ. So tell me now, if you please, whether this grace which is given for the salvation of all is from man or from God? If you say from man, St Paul, that Vessel of God, will refute you, saying, 'the grace of God our Saviour hath appeared to all men' (Titus 2:11). It is the grace of God, he teaches us, not of poor man. Even if the sacred text did not support it, the very matter itself would teach us, for frail earthly nature cannot provide the means to perpetual and immortal good, nor can anyone give another what he lacks himself, or grant an abundance of anything of which he must admit he himself stands in need. You cannot deny that grace must be a gift of God. It is God who gave it; it is given through Our Lord Jesus Christ, therefore Our Lord Jesus Christ is God. And if he is God, as he is, then she who gave birth to God is *Theotokos*, the Mother of God. Can you be so foolish and blasphemous as to assert the contradictory claim that she from whom God was born is not the Mother of God, when you cannot deny that he who was born is truly God?

Let us see what the Gospels say about about the same gift of the grace of Our Lord: 'grace and truth came by Jesus Christ' (John 1:17). If Christ were a mere man, how could this happen through Christ? If he had only a human nature, as you claim, where did that divine virtue come from? If he was indigent and of the earth, whence his heavenly largesse? For no one can give what he does not possess. If Christ gave divine grace, then he possessed what he gave. No one could support the diversity of these two conditions, so greatly differing from each other, so as to suffer poverty and want at the same time as having largesse to bestow. Thus the Apostle Paul, who knew that all the riches of heavenly treasure were in Christ, writes truly to the Churches, 'The grace of Our Lord Jesus Christ be with you' (I Corinthians 16:23). He had often taught that the same person was God and Christ, and that the whole of divine majesty was in him, that the whole fullness of Divinity was in him bodily, so he was correct to pray for the grace of Christ alone without adding the name of God. [He had often enough taught that the grace of God was the same as that of Christ, so now he prays for the grace of Christ alone in its fullness], for he knows that the whole grace of God was contained in the grace of Christ.

'The grace of Our Lord Jesus Christ be with you', he says. Heretics all, whoever you be, I ask you what St Paul was praying for when he wrote thus to the churches? 'The grace of Our Lord Jesus Christ be with you.' If Jesus Christ was a mere man, then in wishing to give the churches the grace of Christ, he was wishing only for a human grace. In saying, 'The grace of Christ be with you', was he saying may the grace of a man be with you, the grace of the flesh be with you, the grace of physical weakness, of frail humanity? Why indeed did he use the word grace at all, if he wanted no more than the grace of a man? There would be no reason for him to want anything when there was nothing there to desire, no reason to pray that his grace should come upon them, if he did not possess the substance of grace that was wanted. These are foolish and ridiculous arguments; lamentable indeed more than laughable, for things which provoke laughter among the

light minded are matters of grief for the faithful and devout. They
shed tears of charity for your foolish lack of belief; their devotion
brings them to tears because of the lack of devotion of others.

Let us pause for a moment and consider, for this opinion does
not only lack wisdom, but the spirit as well; it is empty of spiritual
wisdom, and a stranger to the saving spirit.

VI. Maybe you will claim that the grace of Our Lord Jesus Christ,
of which the Apostle writes, was not born with him, but was later
infused into him by the descent of divinity. Thus the mere man,
if you think him to be no more than that, Our Lord Jesus Christ,
was not born with God but was later assumed by God, so that
in this way grace and divinity were at some stage granted to that
man. We say nothing different about ourselves, that divine grace
descended with divinity, for the divine grace of God is a bestowal
of his divinity in some way, as well as the largesse of gifts of grace.
Perhaps you think the difference between us and Christ is merely
of time, not of nature, if you imagine that the divinity, which we
say was born with Jesus Christ, was afterwards infused. If you do
deny that the divinity was born with Our Lord, you cannot make
a true profession of faith in any further point, for one opinion
cannot be partly impious and partly holy, partly faithful and partly
unfaithful.

I will therefore ask you this first: do you say that Our Lord
Jesus Christ, who was born of the Virgin Mary, was merely the
son of a human being, or really the Son of God? We, meaning the
united faith of the Catholics, we believe both, I say; we understand,
recognize and confess that he is both the Son of Man, being
born of a human being, and the Son of God, being conceived
by the Godhead. So do you admit that he is the Son of God and
of Man, or do you assert he is merely the Son of Man? If so, the
apostles cry out against you, as do the prophets; nay the Holy
Spirit himself cries out, for by him did that conception occur. Your
arrogant lips are stopped up by the united evidence of divinity;
by the sacred witness of Holy Scripture, by the very Gospel of
God as if by the hand of God itself. The great Gabriel himself,

who stopped up the incredulous voice of Zachary by the power of his words, condemned your impious blasphemy much more strongly with what he said to Mary, the virgin Mother of God: 'the Holy Ghost shall come upon thee and the power of the Most High shall overshadow thee. And therefore also the Holy which shall be born of thee shall be called the Son of God' (Luke 1:35). Can you not see how Jesus Christ was the son of man according to the flesh, but was proclaimed the Son of God before that? The Virgin Mary is about to give birth to the Lord, as the Holy Spirit descends upon her, and she conceived with the help of the power of the Most High. By this you must understand that the origin of Our Lord and Saviour was that by which he was conceived; since he was born by the descent of the whole fullness of Divinity into the Virgin, he could not be the Son of Man had he not been the Son of God first. The angel of God who was sent to announce that holy birth, after proclaiming the mystery of his conception, gave a name to the one to be born, saying, 'And therefore also the Holy which shall be born of thee shall be called the Son of God' [that is he will be called the son of the one by whose generation he was begotten]. Jesus Christ is therefore the Son of God, for he was begotten by divinity, and conceived from divinity. If he is the Son of God, then without doubt he is God; if he is God, he does not lack the grace of God, for he could not be in any way lacking in what he himself created, for 'grace and truth came by Jesus Christ' (John 1:17).

VII. All grace, therefore, and all virtue, all power and divinity, all the fullness of divine majesty were with him, and were ever in him, whether in heaven or on earth, in the womb and in his birth. Nothing of God was ever lacking to God, for divinity was ever with God, never separated from him by space or time. Everywhere he is God wholly, everywhere perfect, not divided nor altered nor diminished, for no one could ever add anything to God or take anything away; Godhead knows no diminution, neither does it know increase. He was the same on earth as in heaven, the same in lowliness as in the highest, the same in weak humanity as in the majesty of God. Well does the Apostle call Christ's grace the grace of God, for Christ was all that God is; all the strength of God was at once in him when he was conceived as man, all the divinity, the whole fullness of divinity came into him. All the perfection of Godhead came to him from that source whence was his origin. Never was that man without God, for the very fact that he existed was received from God. Whether you like it or no, you cannot deny this first principle, that Our Lord Jesus Christ is the Son of God, for the archangel cries out in the Gospel, 'therefore also the Holy which shall be born of thee shall be called the Son of God' (Luke 1:35). Granted that, you must acknowledge that whatever you read about Christ refers to the Son of God; whatever you read about Our Lord, or about Jesus, refers to the Son of God, for every one of these titles of his cries out that he is the Son of God. Whatever you hear in all these matters, you must recognize the title of divinity, since in everything you must understand him to be the Son of God: debate, if you can, how to separate God from the Son of God!

❖

✠ BOOK THREE ✠

I. The godlike Master of the Churches, writing to the Romans,
opposes, or rather deplores the lack of belief of the Jews who
were his own brethren, using these words: 'I wished myself to be
an anathema from Christ, for my brethren: who are my kinsmen
according to the flesh; who are Israelites; to whom belongeth the
adoption as of children and the glory and the testament and the
giving of the law and the service of God and the promises; whose
are the fathers and of whom is Christ, according to the flesh, who
is over all things, God blessed for ever' (Romans 9:3–5). What
affection did that faithful apostle show, as a loving relative, what
unimaginable charity to be prepared to die for his relations, as
their kin, for his disciples as their master. What was the reason
he was prepared to die? One only—that they might live. And in
what would that life of theirs consist? In this, as he says himself,
that they might come to recognize Christ as God according to the
flesh, born from their own flesh. The Apostle was more grieved
because they did not understand that he was born from Israel,
for they were the ones who should have loved him most because
he was one of them. 'Of whom is Christ,' he says, 'according to
the flesh, who is over all things, God blessed for ever.' He is born
as Christ, he tells them, from their race, according to the flesh,
and he is the same person who will be blessed for ever as God.
You cannot deny that Christ was born of the Jews according to
the flesh: but the same person who was born from them is God.
How can you evade or dispute that? The Apostle proclaims that
Christ, born of Israel according to the flesh, is God. Tell us, then,
when he was not God! 'Of whom is Christ, according to the flesh,

who is over all things, God'—see how the Apostle joins them together, you cannot at all separate the God from the Christ. As St Paul preaches Christ from the Jews, so he confirms that God is in Christ. You must either deny this or admit it. Christ is said to be born of them according to the flesh, but the same person is proclaimed by the Apostle to be God in Christ. In another place, 'God was in Christ, reconciling the world to himself' (II Corinthians 5:19). No one can divide the one from the other: either deny that Christ was born of the Jews, or admit that it was God who was born of the Virgin in Christ, 'who is over all things, God blessed for ever.'

II. The name of God would be enough to indicate the divine majesty to those who are faithful, but by adding, 'over all things, God blessed for ever', he excludes the possibility of any blasphemous lack of faith; lest someone impious assert that the word God is sometimes granted temporarily to men, as a concession through God's dispensation, and use this fact to impugn the fullness of godhead, qualifying God with contentious arguments: for instance God says to Moses, 'I have appointed thee the God of Pharaoh' (Exodus 7:1), or, 'I have said: You are gods' (Psalm 81/2:6). In these cases it is obvious that the name is given by accommodation. In the text, 'I have said', it is simply reporting speech, not specifying a power; in the text, 'I have appointed thee the God of Pharaoh', it is the power of the one who gives that is expressed, not the divinity of the one who receives. It says, 'I have appointed thee', which implies the power of God who appoints, rather than any divine nature in Moses who received the appointment. However when it is said of Our Lord and God Jesus Christ, 'who is over all things, God blessed for ever', the words prove the reality, and the meaning of the words is demonstrated in the title, for the title of God in the Son of God does not indicate a conceded adoption, but his true and proper nature.

III. St Paul also says, 'henceforth we know no man according to the flesh. And if we have known Christ according to the flesh; but

now we know him so no longer' (II Corinthians 5:16). All the words
of Holy Scripture agree well with each other, and even if the actual
words differ, the real meaning is the same in every part. Thus when
it says here, 'if we have known Christ according to the flesh; but
now we know him so no longer', this present text confirms the
one we cited before, where he says, 'Of whom is Christ according
to the flesh, who is over all things, God blessed for ever.' First he
says, 'of whom is Christ according to the flesh', now he posits, 'if
we have known Christ according to the flesh.' There it runs, 'who
is over all things, God', here, 'now we know him so no longer.' The
form of words differs, but there is one meaning: the same person
who was there proclaimed according to the flesh to be born as
God over all things, is here said to be known no longer according
to the flesh. He whom he knows to have been born in the flesh
as God, he acknowledges for ever, therefore not known to him
according to the flesh, since he is 'over all things, God blessed for
ever.' Now he says, 'God over all things', now he says 'we do not
know Christ according to the flesh', for he is that 'God, blessed for
ever.' The doctrine that the apostle proclaims has become more
sublime, rising to a higher level; even though the sense is the same
in both places, he confirms the mystery of perfect faith as if by a
more direct expression. 'And if we have known Christ according
to the flesh; but now we know him so no longer', means that we
knew him before as both man and God, but now as God alone.
Once the weakness of the flesh has passed, we know nothing in
him save divine power, for the whole virtue of the divine majesty
is in him, though the weakness of lowly human nature has ceased.
By this text St Paul expounds the whole secret of the flesh he
assumed, and the perfection of his divinity. In saying, 'if we have
known Christ according to the flesh,' he speaks of the mystery
of God, born in the flesh; by adding, 'now we know him so no
longer', he gives the force of weakness laid aside. The knowledge
of that flesh refers to the truth of his humanity, knowing it no
longer refers to the honour due to his divinity. It is as much as
to say, 'We have known Christ according to the flesh for as long
as he could be known according to the flesh, but now we do not

so know him since he has ceased to be in the flesh.' The nature of his flesh has been transformed into spiritual substance, and that which was once of man is now wholly of God. We do not know Christ according to the flesh, since his bodily weakness has been taken up into his divine majesty, and nothing remains in his sacred body from which weakness of the flesh could be known in him. Whatever was formerly of two natures, has become one substance, for without doubt Christ who was crucified for us because of our weakness now lives wholly in his divine majesty.

IV. St Paul the Apostle preaches this throughout the corpus of his writings; for instance he writes to the Galatians thus: 'Paul, an apostle, not of men, neither by man, but by Jesus Christ and God the Father' (Galatians 1:1). How well those words fit what he said before and what he says now! In the other text he said, 'now we know Christ according to the flesh no longer', now he says, 'not of men, neither by man, but by Jesus Christ.' Here he teaches the same as he did in the former places. In saying he was not sent by men, he is saying, we do not know Christ according to the flesh; in saying that he was sent not by men but by Jesus Christ, not by man but by God. He is not letting the word 'man' be used of him in whom he proclaims the fullness of divinity. After saying, 'I was sent not of men, neither by man, but by Jesus Christ', he adds, 'and God the Father', specifying that he was sent both by God the Father and God the Son. In the mystery of that sacred and inexplicable generation there are two persons, the begetter and the begotten, but there is one power of God who sends him. He says he was sent by God the Father and God the Son, mentioning the number of two persons, but teaching that there is a single power that sends him.

V. St Paul says that he was sent 'by Jesus Christ and by God the Father, who raised him from the dead' (Galatians 1:1). How splendid and admirable this teacher is, who knows Our Lord Jesus Christ as true God, and proclaims him also as true man; he preaches the divine majesty in him always in such a way that he never moves away from confessing the Incarnation. Thus he excludes Marcion's fantasy by teaching the true incarnation, as well as Ebion's inadequacy by proclaiming perfect divinity, eliminating the risk of men believing either of the blasphemous perversions, that Our Lord Jesus Christ is a mere man and not God, or that he is God and not man. The Apostle speaks well in saying that he was sent by God the Father just as he was by God the Son, and immediately adding a confession of the Lord's Incarnation, with the words, 'who raised him from the dead.' He teaches that the true body of the incarnate God was raised from the dead, just as in the text, 'if we have known Christ according to the flesh; but now we know him so no longer.' What he says he knows according to the flesh is that he was raised from the dead. In that he no longer knows him according to the flesh, is that the weakness of the flesh has passed away and that he knows him to be only in the power of God. He is a faithful and appropriate witness to the divinity of the Lord that we teach, for at the beginning of his ministry he was chastised by heaven, so that he might not only believe with mental faith in the majesty of Our Lord Jesus Christ, raised from the dead, but might actually see him with his bodily eyes.

VI. When Paul was defending himself before King Agrippa and the other judges of this world, he said, 'When I was going to Damascus with authority and permission of the chief priests, at midday, O King, I saw in the way a light from heaven, above the brightness of the sun, shining round about me and them that were in company with me. And, when we were all fallen down on the ground, I heard a voice speaking to me in the Hebrew tongue: Saul, Saul, why persecutest thou me? It is hard for thee to kick against the goad. And I said, Who art thou, Lord? And the Lord answered, I am Jesus whom thou persecutest' (Acts 26:12–15). You can see that the Apostle, who saw him in the splendour of his majesty, could truthfully say that he did not know him according to the flesh. But once he had seen the brilliance of that divine light, which he could not bear, and had fallen prostrate, this voice followed, 'Saul, Saul, why persecutest thou me?' When he enquired who it was, the Lord replied thus, indicating his person, 'I am Jesus of Nazareth, whom thou persecutest.'

So now, O heretic, let me ask you, do you believe what the Apostle says of himself, or not? Or if you despise him, do you believe what the Lord says of himself, or not? If you believe, the case is ended, for it must follow that you would believe as we do. For like the Apostle, we too, even 'if we have known Christ according to the flesh; now we know him so no longer.' We do not insult Christ, we do not separate the flesh from God, we believe that everything that Christ is, is in God. If then you do believe what we believe, you are bound to admit the same mysteries of faith. But if you differ from us, if you do not believe what the Church says, or the Apostle, or God himself says about himself, show us in St Paul's vision which was the flesh and which was God. I cannot distinguish anything here: I see an indescribable light, I see boundless clarity, I see a brilliance which human weakness cannot bear, and beyond what mortal eyes can tolerate; I see the majesty of the limitless God, shining with light. What division is there here, what distinction? We hear the voice name Jesus, we see the majesty of God. How can we avoid believing that God and Jesus were in the one substance?

I would like to say more about this to you. Tell me, I ask, imagine you were now persecuting the Catholic faith, and there appeared to you what appeared to the Apostle in his ignorance, if that brilliance enclosed you, careless in your wrong-headedness, and the splendour of unbounded light struck you down and terrified you, so that you were lying in the darkness of error, and deprived of sight, a darkness made all the greater by unspeakable terror! Tell me, then, if the fear of imminent death were to lie upon you, and the dread of offended majesty were to crush you, and you were to hear yourself called by a name fitting for your lack of faith, while you were in such confusion of mind, 'Saul, Saul, why persecutest thou me?' If you then asked who it was, and heaven replied to you, 'I am Jesus, whom thou persecutest', what could you say? 'I do not know; I do not yet believe enough, I would like to take time to think out who you are, who are speaking to me

from heaven, who are blinding me with divine light, whose voice
I hear, whose majesty I cannot bear. I must consider the matter,
whether to believe you or not. Are you Christ, or God? If you are
only God, are you in Christ? If you are merely Christ, are you in
God? I would like to examine the distinction carefully and think
it through, so as to know what to believe you to be, how to assess
you. I do not want to waste my time by giving you any divine
honours if instead I am to despise you as a mere man!'

St Paul the Apostle fell on his face; if you were prostrated like
him, and were breathless and overwhelmed by the brilliance of
divine light, you might speak like that, you might babble such
an inane response. But what are we to do? The Apostle thought
differently: he lay trembling and faint, but he knew he could
pretend no longer, he had no thought of slow deliberation; it was
enough for him to see the irrefutable evidence that he, whom in
his ignorance he had deemed a mere man, was to be recognized as
God. He did not hesitate or delay, he did not prolong his erroneous
opinion by pondering longer without faith; he had heard from
heaven the name of Jesus his Lord, and like an obedient servant,
trembling as if he had been scourged, he replied with the devout
tones of conversion, 'Lord, what wilt thou have me to do?' (Acts
9:6) His faith was ready, his piety rewarded at once. He believed
faithfully in the Lord, who never deserted him; he gave his heart to
Christ, and Christ entered Paul's heart. He says of himself, 'Do you
seek a proof of Christ that speaketh in me?' (II Corinthians 13:3)

VII. Now, heretic, tell me about that text: he whom the Apostle
says spoke in him, was it a man, or God? If a man, how could the
body of one man speak through the heart of another? If God,
then Christ is not a man but God, for if Christ spoke through the
Apostle, and only God could so speak in him, then the Christ who
speaks in him is God. Do you not see that you have no further case:
there cannot be any disjunction or division between Christ and
God, for God is wholly in Christ, and Christ is wholly in God. We
cannot accept any distinction here, any separation. There is only
one simple article of faith, one that is devout and sensible, namely

to adore, love and worship Christ as God. Do you want fuller and more ample evidence that there is no distinction between Christ and God? To understand that the same person is really God and Christ? Hear the Apostle speaking to the Corinthians: 'We must all be manifest before the judgment seat of Christ, that every one may receive the proper things of the body, according as he hath done, whether it be good or evil' (II Corinthians 5:10). In another place he writes to the Church of Rome, 'we shall all stand before the judgment seat of God' (Romans 14:10). And it is written, 'I have sworn by myself, says the Lord, for every knee shall be bowed to me: and every tongue shall swear' (Isaiah 45:23–4). Do you see now that the coming tribunal of God and the tribunal of Christ are one and the same? So you must understand that Christ is God, for where you see the substance of Christ and God to be quite inseparable, you must acknowledge that they are also inseparable as to the person. Unless, of course, St Paul meant in one epistle that we would be brought before the tribunal of Christ, and in another before that of God, making two tribunals, so that some would be judged by Christ and others by God! This is absurd and frivolous, quite insane. Acknowledge, then, the Lord of all, the God of the universe, the tribunal of Christ in the tribunal of God, the tribunal of God in the tribunal of Christ. Choose life, choose salvation, love the one who created you, and fear him by whom you shall be judged. Whether you will or no, you shall be brought before the tribunal of Christ, you will have to set aside your impious blasphemy and faithless arguments. If you imagine the tribunal of Christ to be other than that of God, you will come before the tribunal of Christ and discover by irrefutable proof that it is the same as the tribunal of God, and that in Christ the Son of God dwells the whole majesty of God the Son and the power of God the Father. 'For neither doth the Father judge any man; but hath given all judgment to the Son, that all men may honour the Son, as they honour the Father' (John 5:22–3). To deny the Father is to deny the Son, 'whosoever denieth the Son, the same hath not the Father. He that confesseth the Son hath the Father also' (I John 5:23).

Learn then that the honour of Father and Son is inseparable, their dignity indivisible. You cannot honour the Son without the Father, nor the Father without the Son. No one can in fact honour God and the Son of God, except in Christ the only-begotten Son of God, for it is only in the Spirit of Christ that we can have the Spirit of the God we want to honour. As St Paul says, 'You are not in the flesh, but in the spirit, if so be that the Spirit of God dwell in you. Now if any man have not the Spirit of Christ, he is none of his.' And further on, 'Who shall accuse against the elect of God? God is he that justifieth. Who is he that shall condemn? Christ Jesus that died; yea that is risen again also' (Romans 8:9, 33–4). You see now, like it or not, that there is no distinction at all between the Spirit of God and the Spirit of Christ, between the judgment of God and the judgment of Christ. Choose which you prefer, for choose one you must: do you understand in faith that Christ is God, or do you recognize Christ in God at your own condemnation?

VIII. Let us see what follows. In writing to the Corinthians, Paul the teacher of all nations says the same thing as we have described already. 'The Jews require signs; and the Greeks seek after wisdom. But we preach Christ crucified; unto the Jews indeed a stumbling-block, and unto the Gentiles foolishness; but unto them that are called, both Jews and Greeks, Christ, the power of God and the wisdom of God' (I Corinthians 1:22–4). What a mighty teacher of the faith! In teaching the Churches he considered it not enough to name Christ as God in this passage unless he added that he was crucified; thus he predicated the wisdom of God to the one whom he called the crucified, to strengthen and confirm the true faith he taught. He used no subtle ambiguities, and he was not ashamed of naming the cross of Christ when he proclaimed the gospel of the Lord. Maybe it was a stumbling block for the Jews, maybe the Gentiles did think it foolishness, to hear that God was born, that God has a body, that God suffered, that God was crucified. He did not water down the strength of his devotion because the Jews did not believe it and found it a difficulty; nor did he lessen the strength of his faith because the Gentiles scoffed and called it foolish. No, he proclaimed openly, consistently and courageously that the power and the wisdom of God are in him whom his mother brought forth, whom men put to death, whom the lance pierced, whom the cross distended; a scandal to the Jews, a folly to the Gentiles! But though scandal or folly it might be to some, to others it is the power and the wisdom of God. As people differ, so their understanding differs; if the faithless fool denies it, wanting sound intellect and unaware of the true good, the wise man knows faithfully in the depths of his heart that it is a sacred and saving truth.

IX. So tell me now, O heretic—you enemy of everyone but especially of yourself, you to whom the Cross of Our Lord Jesus Christ is a scandal, as to the Jews, a folly, as to the Gentiles, you that reject the mystery of true salvation as a scandal to the one, and are not as wise as the others in their folly—why was the preaching of St Paul the Apostle thought madness by the pagans, a stumbling-block to the Jews? If he had taught that Christ was a mere man, as you suppose, what offence would that be to anyone? Who would have found it incredible or difficult that he had been born, suffered on the Cross and died? In what would St Paul's preaching have been novel or unusual if he had said that Christ, an ordinary man, had suffered, since human nature tolerates suffering in other men every day? No, what it was that the foolish Gentiles could not accept, what the unbelieving Jews repudiated, was that the Apostle named Christ, whom they as well as you thought a mere man, and called him truly God. This was what the impious found incredible, what the ears of the unbelievers could not tolerate, that the Apostle preached that God was born, God suffered, God was crucified, in the man Jesus Christ. This was difficult, this was incredible, this was impossible for men to believe, for this had never been heard said of the divine nature. You, then, can be safe in proclaiming your doctrine, since what you say will not be thought foolish by the pagans, will be no difficulty for the Jews. You will not suffer at the hands of Jews or Gentiles, not crucified like Peter, not stoned like James, not beheaded like Paul. Your preaching will cause no offence: you proclaim that a mere man was born, that a mere man died. You need fear nothing: they will not trouble you with persecution, for your preaching confirms their belief!

X. Let us look at the matter again in itself. According to the Apostle, Christ is the power and the wisdom of God. What answer do you make to that? What can you reply? You have no way out, no escape. Christ is the wisdom of God, and the power of God. The one whom the Jews persecuted, whom the Gentiles derided, whom you persecute also with them—he who is foolishness to the pagans and a scandal to the Jews, he, I tell you, is the power and the wisdom of God. What can you do about it? Surely you will not dare to stop your ears, for that is what the Jews did when the Apostle preached! Whatever you try, Christ is now in heaven, in God and with God; he exists on high in him in whom he existed when he was here below. You can no longer join the Jews in persecuting him, but you are doing all you can: you are persecuting him in the Faith, in the Church; you are persecuting with the weapons of evil teaching, with the sword of perverted doctrine. In fact you are doing more than the Jews did of old, for you are persecuting Christ now, whereas they who persecuted him then did afterwards believe. But perhaps you imagine there is less offence in that you cannot now lay hands on him? Not at all, I tell you, this persecution is no less grievous, for you wicked men persecute him in his own people. If hearing of the Cross of the Lord offends you, it was even an offence to the Jews. If you shudder to hear of God suffering, the pagans always mocked at that. I ask you, then, how do you differ from them, when the same perversity affects both you and them? But I will not diminish at all what I preach about the holy Cross, what I proclaim about the suffering of the Lord; no, I will amplify it as far as I possibly can. This man, then, who was crucified, I will proclaim to be the power and the wisdom of God, and there is nothing greater that that, but I will go on to affirm that he is Lord of all divinity and majesty. What I say is the teaching of God himself, for St Paul tells us, 'We speak wisdom among the perfect; yet not the wisdom of this world, neither of the princes of this world that come to nought. But we speak the wisdom of God in a mystery, a wisdom which is hidden, which God ordained before the world, unto our glory; which none of the princes of this world knew. For, if they had known it, they would never have crucified the Lord of glory. But as it is written, That eye hath not seen, nor ear heard, neither hath it entered into the heart of man, what things God hath prepared for them that love him' (II Corinthians 2:6–9, cf. Isaiah 64:4).

Do you see how much the Apostle says in so few words? He says he is speaking wisdom, but a wisdom which only the perfect can know, and the wise men of this age are ignorant of it. It is the wisdom of God, he tells us, which was concealed as a divine secret, intended from before all ages for the glory of the saints. Only those who share the wisdom of God know it, it is quite unknown to the rulers of this age. He gives also the reason for it, to confirm both his statements: 'if they had known it, they would never have crucified the Lord of glory. But as it is written, That eye hath not seen, nor ear heard, neither hath it entered into the heart of man, what things God hath prepared for them that love him.' Do you understand how the wisdom of God, which was hidden in secret, but purposed from before the ages, was unknown to them who did crucify the Lord of glory? Yet it was known to those who received him. Aptly does he say that the wisdom of God was hidden in secret, for no man's eye had ever before seen, nor had ear heard, nor had the heart understood that the Lord of majesty would come to be born of a Virgin, would come to us in the flesh, would be afflicted by every sort of pain and shame. No one was able of his own ability to know these things about God which were hidden in secret, but what bliss for those who know them from revelation! Those who do not recognize these truths must be classed among the rulers of this age; those who know them among the wise men of God. He who denies it does not know God born in the flesh—so you too, who deny it, are among those who do not know him. We will put our trust in the Apostle, whatever you do, and however you impiously deny it. Why do I say Apostle? No, we put our trust in God! It is he whom we believe through the Apostle, for we are sure that he speaks in the Apostle. It is the Word of God that tells us the Lord of majesty was crucified by the rulers of this age; you deny it, as those who crucified him deny that it was God whom they crucified. Those who confess the truth have a share with the Apostle who confessed it: but you must take your share with the persecutors. What more could be said now? The Apostle says they crucified the Lord of majesty: change that if you can, separate Jesus from God if you are able. You cannot surely deny that Christ was crucified by the Jews—but it was the Lord of majesty who was crucified, therefore you must either deny that Christ was fastened to the Cross, or admit that it was God who was so fastened.

XI. But maybe you take exception to our having spoken so long about one text of St Paul, however important. For me the one whom God chose is good enough; I do not blush to take as my witness of faith the one whom God wished to be the teacher of the whole world. But to pander to your whim, since you seem to think there are no other texts I could use, hear the whole mystery of human salvation and eternal bliss, expounded by Martha in the Gospel. What does she say? 'Yea, Lord, I have believed that thou art Christ, the Son of the living God, who art come into this world' (John 11:27). Learn the true faith from a woman, learn to confess eternal hope. You can console yourself with the thought that you need not be ashamed to learn the secret of salvation from a woman, for God himself did not refuse to hear her say it.

XII. Nevertheless, you may insist on the authority of a more distinguished person, even though no one should take offence at any person, male or female, whose authority is conferred by their confession of faith, for the strength of the faith cannot be diminished no matter how humble anyone's place or condition. We will not then enquire of a newly-baptised child who is still not fully instructed, nor of a woman who is only perhaps beginning to come to faith—no, we will ask the greatest one of all, a disciple among the disciples, a master among the masters, he who governs the Roman Church, and enjoys the supremacy among the episcopate that he does in the faith! Tell us, then, tell us, we ask, Peter, Prince of the Apostles, tell us what the Church of God should believe! It is fitting that you, that were taught by the Lord, should teach us; you that have received the keys should open to us the door. Keep away all those who are tunnelling into the mansion of heaven, repel those who are trying to enter through adulterous mines and unlawful passages; for it is certain that no one may enter the gateway to the kingdom, unless it be opened by the key which you have entrusted to the Church. So tell us what we should believe of Jesus Christ, how we should confess him as Lord of all. Doubtless you will reply to us, 'Why ask me how to confess the Lord, when you know how I confessed him myself? Read the Gospel: you do not need me in person, since you have my profession of faith. Rather, you have me in person once you have my profession, since my person has no authority apart from that profession, and the authority of my person stems from that profession itself.'

So, then, Evangelist, tell us that profession; tell us the faith of the chief apostle: did he confess Jesus to be man alone, or God? Did he only proclaim the flesh in him, or the Son of God? For when Our Lord Jesus Christ asked the disciples who they believed in, and what they believed him to be, Peter replied as the leader of the apostles, one speaking for all. The reply made by the one was the same as what all believed, but it was fitting for the leader to reply, so that the order of precedence might be preserved in their reply. He who was the senior in age spoke before the others: what did he say? 'Thou art Christ, the Son of the Living God' (Matthew 16:16).

To refute you, O heretic, I must question you in a simple and rustic manner: so, let me ask, who was it to whom Peter was responding? You cannot deny that it was Christ. I ask, then, what do you call Christ, man or God? A man, without doubt, for that is the source of your heresy in denying Christ to be the Son of God. That is why you assert that Mary is only the *Christotokos*, not *Theotokos*; being the Mother only of Christ, not of God. In asserting that Christ is only a man and not God, it follows that he is only the son of man, and not of God. But what does St Peter say to this? 'Thou art Christ, the Son of the Living God.' You claim that this Christ is merely the son of man, but he says that he is the Son of God. Which am I to believe, you or St Peter? I do not imagine you are so arrogant as to put yourself before the prince of the apostles! But what is the limit of your audacity? How can you fail to despise the apostle, since you have found yourself able to contradict God? St Peter said, 'Thou art Christ, the Son of the Living God.' Is there any room for ambiguity or obscurity in that? It is a simple and straightforward profession, to proclaim Christ as Son of God.

Maybe you deny it was ever said: but we have the word of the evangelist. Or do you claim that an apostle was lying? That would be a vile falsehood, to accuse an apostle of deceit. Or maybe you think that the words were spoken about some other Christ? That would be a prodigiously novel interpretation. What remains? Only this, since you can read what was written, and what was written is true, you are compelled to admit that it cannot be false, you must cease from impugning the truth.

XIII. I have cited the evidence of the chief of the apostles, the confession he made of his faith that Our Lord Jesus Christ is God, in the very presence of Christ; now let us see how the one he confessed showed his approval of that confession, since if God himself gave his approval that counts for much more than the word of the Apostle. When St Peter said, 'Thou art Christ, the Son of the Living God', what did Our Lord and Saviour reply? He said, 'Blessed art thou, Simon Bar-Jona; because flesh and blood hath not revealed it to thee, but the Spirit of my Father, who is in heaven' (Matthew 16:17). If you are not pleased that I use the evidence of an apostle, use that of God. In praising what was said, God adds his own authority to that of the apostle; thus though the words were spoken by the lips of the apostle, God made them his own by approving them. 'Blessed art thou, Simon Bar-Jona; because flesh and blood hath not revealed it to thee, but the Spirit of my Father, who is in heaven.' You see in what the apostle said the evidence of the Holy Spirit; of the Son who was present, and of God the Father. What more then could you require, what confirmation? The Son gave his praise, the Father was present, the Holy Spirit revealed. What St Peter said was the evidence of the whole of the Godhead, since the words must have the authority of the one from whom they proceeded. 'Blessed art thou, Simon Bar-Jona; because flesh and blood hath not revealed it to thee, but the Spirit of my Father, who is in heaven.' If it was not flesh and blood that revealed these things to Peter, and inspired him, understand now who is your own inspiration. If it was the Spirit of God who taught him to confess Christ as God, see now that it is the spirit of the devil who teaches you to deny him.

XIV. Now what followed after the words in which the Lord commended Peter? What did he say next? 'And I say to thee that: Thou art Peter; and upon this rock I will build my Church.' Do you understand that what Peter said is the faith of the Church? And he who does not hold the faith of the Church must be outside the Church. 'And I will give to thee the keys of the kingdom of heaven.' That faith merited heaven, that faith received the keys of the kingdom of heaven. See what remains for you: you cannot enter that gate to which this is the key, if you deny the faith of that key. 'And the gates of hell shall not prevail against it.' By the gates of hell he means the belief of heretics, or rather their lack of belief. As far as heaven is distant from hell, so far distant from him who denies it is he who confesses that Christ is God. 'And whatsoever that shalt bind upon earth, it shall be bound also in heaven; and whatsoever thou shalt loose on earth, it shall be loosed also in heaven.' The perfect faith of the apostle received in some way the power of divinity, so that what he bound or loosed on earth should be bound or loosed in heaven. But you, if you go against the faith of the apostle, will see yourself bound on earth, and must therefore know that you will be bound in heaven.

But it is a long business to go through every text, since they are so many that they would make our discourse too bulky and verbose, even if we quote them briefly and succinctly.

XV. Nevertheless I would like to add one more apostolic witness, so that you may understand that what was done before Our Lord's passion was in accordance with what followed after his passion. When Our Lord appeared among his disciples, the doors being closed, he wished to demonstrate the reality of his body to the apostles. St Thomas the apostle touched his flesh, felt his side, probed his wounds; when he had investigated the truth of the body that had appeared to him, what did he exclaim? 'My Lord and my God' (John 20:28). Did he say what you say, a man and not God, Christ alone, not the divinity? He touched the body of his Lord, and called him God. Did he make any further distinction between man and God? Did he call that flesh merely the *Theodochos,* the image that receives Divinity, as you assert? Did he declare, in your manner, that the one he was touching was not to be revered for his own sake but only for the sake of the one he had received into himself? But surely God's apostle was innocent of such a subtle distinction, unaware of your precise assessment of the difference, since he was a countryman, uneducated, ignorant of the art of dialectic and the techniques of philosophy; for him the teaching of his Lord was good enough; for he knew nothing except what he had learned through the Lord's instruction. His words were heavenly in their inspiration, his faith had the authority of God; he had never learned to separate his Lord from his own body, as you do, nor to divide God from himself.

He was holy, sincere, loving and possessed of innocence with experience, undamaged faith, incorrupt knowledge. He had a simple understanding, but with acuteness, wisdom, with perfect simplicity. He was untainted by any evil, free from all corruption, immune from any perverse heresy; he reflected the form of divine majesty in himself, and held firm only to what he had learnt. You may think he was an uneducated rustic, but he refutes you by his brief response, destroys you in a few words. What was it that the apostle Thomas touched, when he came to feel God? It was Christ, without doubt. And what did he exclaim? 'My Lord and my God!' Now separate Christ from God if you can, change those words if you are able. Use all the tricks of dialectic, your worldly wisdom, your foolish philosophy based on quibbles over words. Turn everything back to front and contradict yourself! But whatever your mind or skill can do, whatever you may do or say, you will never be able to elude the conclusion, you must admit that what the apostle actually touched was God. Maybe you would like to find some way to change the record in the Gospel, so that it might read that the Apostle Thomas did not touch the Lord's body, or say that Christ was Lord and God, but no, you cannot change what is written in the Gospels of God. 'Heaven and earth shall pass; but my words shall not pass' (Matthew 24:35). See even now the one who gave witness cries out to you, Thomas the Apostle cries out, 'Jesus whom I touched is God, it is God whose limbs I have felt. I did not take hold of something incorporeal, I did not touch something that was not solid; it was not a spirit that I felt with my hand, that I might be believed to have said of it 'It is God', for as my Lord himself said, 'a spirit hath not flesh and bones' (Luke 24:39). I touched the body of my Lord, I felt his flesh and bones, I placed my finger in the place of his wounds, and I proclaimed of Christ my Lord that he is 'My Lord and my God.' I knew of no distance to place between Christ and God, I wish to insert no sacrilegious distinction between Jesus and God, I have no intention of dividing my Lord from himself. Depart from me, anyone who thinks differently, and anyone who says anything different! I know no other Christ than God, this I and my fellow apostles have held, this I have taught to the Churches, this I preached to the pagans, this I cry out to you as well, Christ is God, Christ is God.' No sane mind can think otherwise, no true faith can say differently, Divinity cannot be divided from itself. Whatever is of Christ is of God, and in God can be found nothing but what is of God.

XVI. So what have you to say for yourself now, O heretic? Are these witnesses to the faith enough for you, so lacking in faith, or should we add something more? What could we add, after the prophets and apostles, unless perhaps you demand that a sign from heaven be given you, as the Jews once asked? If that is what you want, I must give you the answer given to them: 'An evil and adulterous generation seeketh a sign; and a sign shall not be given it, but the sign of Jonas the prophet' (Matthew 12:39). That sign should be enough for you, as it was for the Jews who crucified him, that you should believe Our Lord to be God by the very fact that those who had persecuted him came to believe. But since we have mentioned signs from heaven, I will give you a sign from heaven: one, moreover, which the devils themselves cannot deny, for they were forced by the truth of the matter to cry out that the same Jesus whom they saw in the flesh is God. What does the Gospel say about the Lord Jesus Christ? 'And Jesus, being baptized, forthwith came out of the water; and lo, the heavens were opened to him, and he saw the Spirit of God descending as a dove and coming upon him. And behold, a voice from heaven, saying: This is my beloved son, in whom I am well pleased' (Matthew 3:16–17).

What do you say to that, O heretic? Is it what was said that you dislike, or the one who said it? The meaning of what was said needs no interpretation, the dignity of the speaker needs no recommendation. It was God the Father who spoke: what he said is clear. Dare you utter the sacrilegious and impudent thought that you need not even believe what God the Father says about the only begotten Son of God? 'This is my beloved son, in whom I am well pleased.' Perhaps you will attempt to say that these words were spoken only of the Word and not of Christ? What madness! Tell me, who was being baptized, the Word, or Christ? Flesh, or spirit? You cannot deny that it was Christ. He was a man, born of man and also of God, for the Holy Spirit came down to the Virgin, and he was conceived by the power of the most high that overshadowed her; he is thus son of man and son of God—he is the one, and you cannot deny it, who was baptized. If he was the one baptized, then he was the one named; he who was named was the one who was baptized. 'This is my beloved son, in whom I am well pleased.' Could anything more profound be said, or more clearly? Christ was baptized; Christ came out of the water; to the baptized Christ were the heavens opened, for the sake of Christ the dove descended upon Christ; the Holy Spirit was there in bodily form, and the Father called on Christ. Now if you are so bold as to deny that these words were spoken of Christ, it remains that Christ was not baptized, nor did the Spirit descend, nor did the Father speak. But the truth presses on you and forces you, even if you are unwilling to admit the truth, at least not to deny it. For what did the evangelist say? 'And Jesus, being baptized, forthwith came out of the water.' Who was baptized? Surely Christ. 'And lo, the heavens were opened to him.' To whom? Surely the one who had been baptized, Christ in fact. 'And he saw the Spirit of God descending as a dove and coming upon him.' Who saw it? Christ, indeed. And on whom did he descend? On Christ without doubt. 'And behold, a voice from heaven, saying.' Speaking of whom? Of Christ. And what follows? 'This is my beloved son, in whom I am well pleased.' The voice concludes in order to show us for whose benefit all these things happened, the voice that said, 'This is my beloved son.' This is as much as to say, 'This is he for whom all these things happened. This is my Son, for whom the heavens opened, for whose sake my Spirit came down, for whom my own voice spoke. This then is my Son.' And in saying, 'This is my Son', whom did he mean? Surely the one on whom the dove rested. On whom did the dove rest? On Christ. Therefore Christ is the Son of God. I think my case is complete.

Now, heretic, do you understand that a sign has been given you from heaven? Not one sign, indeed, but many remarkable ones. You find one in the opening of heaven, another in the descent of the Spirit, a third in the voice of the Father. And all of these declare Christ most plainly to be God. The opening of the heavens indicates him to be God. The descent of the Holy Spirit ratifies his divinity. The voice of the Father confirms that he is God. For the heavens would never have opened except to honour their Lord; the Spirit would not have come down in bodily form except on the Son of God; the Father would not have called anyone his Son except his true Son. These indications of his divine origin do not only confirm the truth of our pious faith, but also exclude all wicked and false unbelief. The splendour of the ineffable voice of God claims paternity clearly and specifically, saying, 'This is my beloved son', and proceeds in the words that follow to proclaim his love, 'my beloved son in whom I am well pleased.' Just as the prophet preached God both strong and great, so now he says, 'This is my beloved son, in whom I am well pleased.' He calls his own Son by the name of beloved, and adds that of well-pleasing, so that the added titles might indicate his true divine nature, and grant to the Son of God a degree of honour that could never be applied to any mere human being. These things were granted personally and uniquely to the person of Our Lord Jesus Christ; for him the heavens opened, and God the Father as it were touched him with his hand in the dove that appeared and rested upon him, before the gaze of all, and pointed him out with the finger of his right hand, saying, 'This is my beloved son.' He was indicated by the special personal attribute of being well beloved, and in a particular way pleasing to the Father; the unique occurrences demonstrated his unique nature, and the specific title of only-begotten Son specified the reality of that nature which the preceding signs had indicated.

Now here let us make an end of this section. These words of God the Father cannot be improved on or equalled by anything we can say. It is enough for us that God the Father is the witness for our Lord Jesus Christ, in saying, 'This is my Son.' If you think you can contradict those words of God the Father, you are contradicting the one who made the whole world acknowledge his Son by the most compelling of evidence.

❖

✠ BOOK FOUR ✠

I. We have used up three books in a wealth of trustworthy texts, since truth speaks not in human words alone but in the words of God; these texts are more than enough for us to prove our cause through divine authority, for God's authority is surely adequate to prove his own case. In fact the whole corpus of sacred writings is full of such evidence, for there are as many teachings as witnesses, but in fact Holy Scripture gives a single body of evidence, spoken by the mouth of God. We thought it necessary to collect so many texts not because it was necessary for our proof, but to make it easier through their abundance. Thus anything that was superfluous to our defence might serve to adorn the whole.

In the previous three books, then, we have proved that Our Lord Jesus Christ was God while he was on earth and in the flesh, not only through the evidence of prophets and apostles, but of evangelists and angels as well. Now we will demonstrate how he who was born in the flesh was always God even before he took flesh. As the evidence of the holy Scriptures concurs and cries out together, you may understand that you must believe that the same person who in his physical birth was God and man, was God alone before his physical nativity. He who was God incarnate after the Virgin gave birth was God the Word before she gave birth. Learn therefore from the Apostle, the Teacher of the whole world, that he who is God without any beginning, God the Son, was made the Son of Man at the end of the world, that is to say in the fullness of time. For he says, 'When the fulness of the time was come, God sent his Son, made of a woman, made under the Law' (Galatians 4:4). Tell me now, before Our Lord Jesus Christ was born of his mother Mary, did God have a Son, or not? You cannot deny that he had, for there could never be a son without a father, or a father without a son; thus as the son is so named in relation to his father, so is the father in relation to the son.

II. You can see that the Apostle says that God sent his Son; his Son indeed, God sent his own Son in the very words of the Apostle. It was not any other son that he sent, for it was his own that we are told he sent, nor could he send at all unless there were one to be sent. He sent, therefore, his own Son, made of a woman. If then he sent him, he sent one who existed; he sent his own, not any other, but his own did he send. So what comes of your earthly and naive argument, that 'No one gives birth to one older than herself.' Is not the Lord older than Mary? Is not the Son of God older than the daughter of man? Is not God older than mankind itself? For there is no man who does not come from God. You can see, then, that Mary did indeed give birth to one older than herself, not only older, I tell you, but the one who made her; she procreated her own creator; she was the mother of her father. It was as easy for God to arrange his own birth as it had been to arrange any human birth; as easy to make himself born as for any man to be born. For the power of God is not limited with regard to his own person, as if what he may do for all others he cannot do for himself, as if it were in the nature of divinity that God should be able to do all things, but he should not be able in his own person to be God in man. Let us set aside all these frivolous and passing earthly arguments and quibbles! Let us believe the simple evidence of the naked truth. Let us put our trust in the evidence of those whom God sent, of those in whom he spoke about himself, if I may put it thus. It is right that we should believe him when he speaks of himself, since it is from him that we know all that we do know about him. God could not be known by man at all, did he not himself grant that knowledge. It is right that we should believe everything that we know about him, since all that knowledge comes from him, for if we believe not him from whom comes our knowledge, it would follow that we knew nothing at all, if we do not believe the source of knowledge.

III. From the text I have quoted it is clear that God sent his own Son, and he was made the son of man, who had always been the Son of God. Now let us look to see if the same Apostle said anything else of a similar nature, so that the truth, which shines of itself, may shine even brighter at the evidence of two witnesses. St Paul says, therefore, 'God sent his own Son in the likeness of sinful flesh' (Romans 8:3). You understand that the Apostle said nothing casually or without intending it, as if he would contradict what he had once said? Indeed no chance or inconsidered word could fall from him, for he enjoyed the fullness of divine counsel and speech. He then who said, 'God sent his own Son in the likeness of sinful flesh', repeats the same teaching that God sent his Son. What a marvellous and noble master he is, for he knew that the whole mystery of the Catholic faith was contained in this point, that we believe the Lord was born in the flesh and the Son of God was sent into this world. This he cries out again and again, saying, 'God sent his Son.' He was sent in particular to proclaim the gospel of the coming of God, so we should not be surprised if he teaches this, given that the very Lawgiver cried out the same, even before there was a Law, saying, 'I beseech thee, Lord, send whom thou sendest'. It is much clearer in the Hebrew manuscripts, which read, 'I beseech thee, Lord, send whom thou wilt send' (Exodus 4:13). The holy prophet speaks of the desire of the whole human race, he who is to be sent by the Father for the redemption and salvation of all, and he longs for him to be sent speedily, calling to God the Father in the name of all human flesh, and saying, 'I beseech thee, Lord, send whom thou wilt send.' 'God sent his own Son in the likeness of sinful flesh.' He says well that he was sent in the flesh, but excluding any sin in that flesh. For in saying, 'God sent his own Son in the likeness of sinful flesh', he intends us to understand that the flesh was real enough, but there was no reality of sin. Truth should be predicated of the flesh, likeness only of the sin. For all flesh is sinful, except that he had flesh without sin. He had the likeness of sinful flesh, while he was in the flesh, but he lacked the reality of sin, for he was without sin. Hence he says, 'God sent his own Son in the likeness of sinful flesh.'

IV. Do you want to know how aptly the Apostle taught? Hear how these words came from the mouth of the Apostle as if from the very mouth of God: the Lord said, 'God sent not his Son into the world to judge the world; but that the world may be saved by him' (John 3:17). The Lord himself, as you can see, claims to have been sent by God the Father for the salvation of mankind. Now if you think it should have been made clearer which Son God sent for the salvation of mankind, as if God had not one only true and begotten Son, when it says that he sent his son, it is also made clear that it was his only-begotten son. Hear the prophet David, making it very clear who was to be sent for man's salvation: 'He sent his Word, and healed them' (Psalm 106/7:20). Can you give that a fleshly meaning? Can you say that God sent a mere man to heal the human race? Surely not: David in his prophecy, along with the whole of Scripture, refutes you saying, 'He sent his Word, and healed them.' You can see that the Word was sent by God to save mankind, for as it was Christ through whom salvation was granted, it was the Word of God in Christ which saved all things through Christ. Christ and the Word of God were united in the mystery of the incarnation, so that Christ and the Word of God became the one Son of God out of the two natures. The Apostle John wanted to make this clear, and wrote, 'The Father hath sent his Son, to be the Saviour of the World' (I John 4:14). Do you see how he conjoined God and man in an inseparable union? Christ, who was born of Mary, is called Saviour without ambiguity, as in the text, 'For this day is born to you a Saviour, who is Christ the Lord' (Luke 2:11). And here he names the Saviour, identified with the Word of God that was sent, saying, 'God sent his Son, to be the Saviour of the World.'

V. It is clear, then, that through the mystery of the Word of God in union with humanity, the Word which was sent for our salvation is called our Saviour, and the Saviour who was born in the flesh is called the Son of God because of the Word united with him. Thus in the dignity of both names, whatever attributes there be of humanity and divinity, he is called God without differentiation, for God is united with mankind. The same Apostle makes this point well, saying, 'Whosoever shall confess that Jesus is the Son of God, God abideth in him, and the charity of God is perfected with us' (I John 4:15, 17). He proclaims that the one who believes that Jesus is the Son of God believes rightly about him, and is therefore full of the love of God. He bears witness that the Word of God is the Son of God, and in this one person he wishes us to recognize both the only-begotten Word of God, and Jesus Christ the Son of God. Can you ask for a clearer explanation of how Christ was born according to the flesh, true man from true man, but because of the ineffable mystery of the union by which that man is united with God, there is no differentiation between Christ and the Word? Hear Our Lord in the Gospels—or rather hear God speaking about himself, 'This is eternal life; that they may know thee, the only true God, and Jesus Christ whom thou hast sent' (John 17:3). You have already heard that the Word of God was sent to save mankind; now you hear that he who was sent is Jesus the Christ. Separate them if you can, since you can see such a unity between Christ and the Word, that not only is the Word united with Christ, but also Christ is called the Word because of that very unity.

VI. Maybe you still think this is insufficiently clear? Not that it is unclear in itself, but dark infidelity can always create darkness for itself even in full daylight. So hear in a few words how the Apostle Paul sums up the whole mystery of the unity of Our Lord: 'There is one Lord Jesus Christ, by whom are all things' (I Corinthians 8:6). O good Jesus, what authority there is in your words! For what is said of you by your own is your own. See how much is contained in those few words of the Apostle! 'There is one Lord Jesus Christ, by whom are all things.' Did he use some complicated verbal formula to set forth this great mystery? Did he spend a long time in rhetoric describing what he wanted us to believe? No, he says, 'There is one Lord Jesus Christ, by whom are all things.' He reveals to us the most majestic secrets in a simple short phrase. He was confident that he did not need to use long speeches in setting forth the matter of God, for the divinity itself would lend credence to his words. To confirm what he said all that was needed was a demonstration of the facts, for the proof lay in the authority of the speaker. 'There is one Lord Jesus Christ,' he says, 'by whom are all things.' Think where you have read the same thing about the Word of the Father that you now read about Christ. The Evangelist says, 'All things were made by him, and without him was made nothing' (John 1:3). The Apostle says all things were made by Christ; the Evangelist says all things were made by the Word. Can Holy Scripture disagree with itself? Surely not; but we are intended to understand that it is of the very same person that the Apostle says all things were made by Christ, and the Evangelist says through the Word were all things made. Hear too what God himself proclaims about the Word of God: 'No man hath ascended into heaven, but he that descended from heaven, the Son of Man who is in heaven' (John 3:13). And in another place, 'If then you shall see the Son of Man ascend up where he was before?' (John 6:63) He tells us that the Son of Man was in heaven; he affirms that the Son of Man descended from heaven. Why murmur more? Deny it if you can! You want proof of what I have said? I will not give it: it was God who spoke, God said these things; for me his own word is the perfect proof. Away with arguments and debates: the person of the speaker is enough for me to believe. I have no right to dispute about the faith, no right to question it. How can I challenge the truth of what God has said? For I cannot doubt that what God has said is the truth. 'No man hath ascended into heaven, but he that descended from heaven, the Son of Man who is in heaven.' Now the Word of the Father was always in heaven; but how can he say that the Son of Man was always in heaven? Learn, then, that he is showing us that the Son of Man is the same person who was always the Son of God, for he tells us that he who has recently become the Son of Man did exist in heaven always. And a greater thing follows from that, for he bears witness that the same Son of Man, that is the Word of God whom he said descended from heaven, was actually in heaven even while he was speaking on

earth. 'No man hath ascended into heaven, but he that descended
from heaven, the Son of Man who is in heaven.' Who is it who
is speaking? Christ. Where was he at the time he was speaking?
On earth. How can he bear witness that he descended from
heaven when he was born, and is actually in heaven while he is
speaking, and says that he is that same Son of Man, when only
God could have descended from heaven, and only the infinity of
God could be speaking upon earth while at the same time being
in heaven. Look at the evidence, and understand; the Son of Man
is the same person as the Word of God, since he is Son of Man
through being really born of a human being, and the Word of
God since he remains in heaven even while he is speaking on
earth. It follows from his human birth that he is truly called the
Son of Man; from his divine infinity that he never departs from
heaven. Thus St Paul speaks, aptly following Our Lord's words,
'He that descended is the same also that ascended above all the
heavens, that he might fill all things' (Ephesians 4:10). The same
person, he says, descended as ascended. No one could descend
from heaven, save for the Word of God. And indeed, he 'being in
the form of God, thought it not robbery to be equal with God;
but emptied himself, taking the form of a servant, being made in
the likeness of men, and in habit found as a man. He humbled
himself, becoming obedient unto death, even to the death of the
cross' (Philippians 2:6–8). The Word of God, then, descended
from heaven; the Son of Man ascended into heaven. St Paul tells
us that the one who descended and the one who ascended were
the same person. You can see, therefore, that the Son of Man is
the same as the Word of God.

VII. We must therefore say, without doubt or fear, and with the
authority of the word of God, that the Son of Man descended from
heaven, and the Lord of majesty was crucified. In the mystery
of the incarnation, the Son of God was made Son of Man, and
the Lord of majesty was crucified in the Son of Man. And what
follows more? It would take too long to say much about every
point; the day would end if I were to attempt to investigate and

explain everything which could be connected to this matter. I would have to turn over every page of Scripture if I wanted to do that, and to read them again, for what passage is there that is irrelevant to this matter, since the whole was written for the sake of it? I must speak briefly, therefore, and concisely if I am to be able to say anything; I must list texts more than explain them, and make up for my deficiencies with more deficiencies, so to speak. Since I must run over quite a number of passages, I shall have to be virtually silent about most of them.

Our Saviour tells us in the Gospel that 'the Son of Man is come to seek and to save that which was lost' (Luke 19:10). St Paul says, 'A faithful saying and worthy of all acceptation: that Christ Jesus came into the world to save sinners, of whom I am the chief' (I Timothy 1:15). John the evangelist adds, 'He came unto his own, and his own received him not' (John 1:11). You can see how the Scriptures tell us in one place that the Son of Man came into the world, in another place Jesus Christ, in a third the Word of God. Understand them that the difference is in titles, not subjects, and under the different names there is the reality of a single person. If it is now the Son of Man, now the Son of God which is the Word who is named as coming into the world, understand that there is one person who is indicated by the two names.

VIII. Now as the evangelist tells us that he through whom the world was made came into the world, and was made the Son of Man, who is God the creator of the world, it does not matter what he is called in particular places, since he is known to be God in all of them. The dignity of God is not prejudiced, nor is his will, since it is a greater proof of his divinity that he became whatever he wanted to be. Since he wished it, he came into the world; because he wanted it, he was born as man, because he willed it, he was called the Son of Man. All of these titles are virtues of God, and the variety of names does not diminish the strength of his power. Whatever is said of him, he is one person in all of them; and whatever diversity you see in the types of name given him, there is only one majestic power in them all.

IX. So far we have mostly used the evidence of the evangelists and apostles, as recent witnesses: now let us add some from the ancient prophets. By mixing old texts with new ones, we shall make everyone understand that Holy Scripture cries out as if with one voice through its entire body that the Lord would come in the flesh. Jeremiah the prophet was remarkable and admirable both in the gifts he received from God and the witness he gave, and he alone was sanctified before he was born: he says, 'This is our Lord, and there shall no other be accounted of in comparison of him. He found out all the way of knowledge and gave it to Jacob his servant and to Israel his beloved. Afterwards he was seen upon earth and conversed with men' (Baruch 3:36–8). This, then, is our God. Can you see how the prophet indicates God, and points his finger to show us him? This is our God. Tell me, which God is the prophet showing us by these indications? Is it not the Father? Why did he need to point him out, when everyone thought they knew him? The Jews were not then ignorant of God, for they lived under the Law of God. No, he did this so that they might know the Son of God to be God. Aptly did the prophet say that he who devised all discipline, in other words gave them the Law, would be seen upon the earth, that is would come in the flesh. Since the Jews had no doubts that he who gave them the law was God, they might recognize that he who was to come in the flesh was God, when they heard that he whom they believed to be their God and lawgiver would be seen among men by taking on flesh. He himself promised that he would come, speaking through another prophet: 'For I myself that spoke, behold, I am here' (Isaiah 52:6). The previous passage said, 'there shall no other be accounted of in comparison of him' (Baruch 3:36). Well did the prophet foresee the perversions of doctrine and exclude any possibility of placing a heretical sense on it, for he said, 'No other shall be accounted of.' He alone was born of God, into Godhead; at his bidding the work of the universe was carried out; at his will things had their beginning; at his command the world was made; he spoke all things, and they were made; he ordered all things, and they were created. He alone it was who spoke to the patriarchs, who dwelt in the prophets; he was conceived of the Spirit, born from the Virgin Mary, seen in the world, dwelling among men; he fastened the accusation of sin to the wood of the cross, and triumphed in himself; by his death he slew our enemies and the powers ranged against us, by his rising he granted faith to all, in his glorified body he put an end to the corruption of human flesh. Can you see how these things are said specifically of Our Lord Jesus Christ? None other is compared with him, for he alone was born, God from God, in this unique glory and bliss. The purpose of the teaching of the prophets is to make the Only-begotten Son of God manifest to all, so that when they hear that no other son is accounted of in comparison with God, they may recognize that there is One God both Father and Son.

'Afterwards he was seen upon earth and conversed with men' (Baruch 3:38). Can you see how clearly the coming and birth of the Lord are indicated? Was the Father ever seen upon earth, he who is only made visible in his Son; did the Father appear in flesh, did he converse with men? No indeed: All these things, you must understand, were spoken of the Son. When the prophet said that God would be seen upon earth, and no person other than the Son has been seen upon earth, we can be sure that the prophet was speaking of none other than the one of whom subsequent events proved what was prophesied. When he said that God would be seen, this could not be spoken truthfully of anyone but the one who was in truth seen later on.

That is enough about that text: let us look at another. 'The labour of Egypt', says Isaiah, 'and the merchandise of Ethiopia, and of Sabaim men of stature, shall come over to thee and shall be thine. They shall walk after thee, they shall go bound with manacles. And they shall worship thee and shall make supplication to thee: Only in thee is God: and there is no God beside thee. Thou art our God, and we knew it not, the God of Israel, the Saviour' (Isaiah 45:14–15, LXX). How well do the divine scriptures agree among themselves! The previous prophet said, 'This is our God', here is said, 'Thou art our God'. In the one is divine teaching, in the other human faith. One is spoken in the person of the Master who teaches, the other in the person of the people who believe. Set the prophet Jeremiah to teach every day in the Church, as he does, saying of Our Lord Jesus Christ, 'This is our God.' What could all the Church reply save what she actually does, as the other prophet said of Our Lord Jesus, 'Thou art our God'? To our present profession of faith can we add the admission of past ignorance, as the people say, 'Thou art our God, and we knew it not.' Those who were so confused by the superstitions of the devil that they were ignorant of God, can now turn to faith and say, 'Thou art our God, and we knew it not.'

X. If you would like this point proved to you from the point of view of the Jews, consider those of the Jewish people who had formerly been unhappy in their ignorance and persecuted wickedly, but turned to faith and acknowledged God: can they not truly say, 'Thou art our God, and we knew it not.' But I will go further: I can show you the example not only of those Jews who believe, but of those who deny Christ. Ask those who persist in the errors of Judaism, whether they know God and believe in him. They will profess that they do know, and do believe. But ask them whether they believe in the Son of God, and they will deny it, with a curse. Was it not of him, therefore, that the prophet said that those Jews were always ignorant of him, and are still ignorant, rather than of him whom they truly know and confess? Those of the Jews who have come to the faith after ignorance can aptly say, 'Thou art our God, and we knew it not.' Those who come to faith out of ignorance can truly say that they knew not the one whom those who still do not believe admit they do not know. It is clear that it is he whom those who believe after ignorance may say that they did not formerly know, he whom those who deny him know not still.

XI. 'The labour of Egypt', says Isaiah, 'and the merchandise of Ethiopia, and of Sabaim men of stature, shall come over to thee' (Isaiah 45:14). By naming these various nations, he indicates the arrival of pagans who will come to believe, that is clear. And no one can deny that the pagans have been converted to Christ, for by adopting the name of Christian, they have changed not only their belief to faith in Our Lord Jesus Christ, but their very name as well. As they changed their name, so did the reality of their faith, in the mystery of that name. 'They shall come over to thee, and shall be thine. They shall walk after thee, they shall go bound with manacles' (*ibid*). As there are bonds which coerce, so there are bonds of charity, as the Lord said, 'I will draw them with the bands of love' (Hosea 11:4). Truly these bonds are great, and the love beyond all telling, for those who are bound rejoice in their bonds. Would you be sure this is true? Hear St Paul the Apostle rejoicing and glad of his bonds, when he says, 'I therefore, a prisoner in the Lord, beseech you' (Ephesians 4:1), and again, 'I beseech thee, whereas thou art such a one, as Paul, an old man and now a prisoner also of Jesus Christ' (Philemon 9). See how he rejoices at having merited such bonds, that he actually encourages others to follow his example. Where the love of the Lord is, there surely also the same love causes us to be bound together, as it is written, 'The multitude of believers had but one heart and one soul' (Acts 4:32).

And Isaiah continues, 'They shall worship thee and shall make supplication to thee: Only in thee is God: and there is no God beside thee' (Isaiah 45:14). The Apostle clearly confirms what the Prophet said, in the words, 'For God indeed was in Christ, reconciling the world to himself' (II Corinthians 5:19). The prophet said, 'only in thee is God: and there is no God beside thee', and rightly does he say 'in thee is God', telling us that not only he who was then present but he who was to come would dwell as one of those among whom he dwelt, distinguishing the two natures without denying the unity of person.

XII. 'Thou art our God', he continues, 'and we knew it not, the God of Israel, the Saviour' (Isaiah 45:15, LXX). Though there are many passages of Scripture which make the point we have been expounding, this is the clearest of all where he names Christ as our Saviour, for Christ is indeed our Saviour, as the angel said, 'For this day is born to you a Saviour, who is Christ the Lord' (Luke 2:11). No one is ignorant that the name Jesus in Hebrew means 'saviour', as the angel announced to the Blessed Virgin Mary, in the words, 'and thou shalt call his name Jesus, for he shall save his people from their sins' (Luke 1:31, Matthew 1: 21). Lest you should imagine that he was announcing a saviour just like others of whom the word was used, such as 'the Lord raised them up a saviour: to wit, Othoniel the son of Cenez', and 'the Lord raised them up a saviour called Aod, the son of Gera' (Judges 3:9, 15), Scripture adds, 'he shall save his people from their sins' (Matthew 1: 21). No mere human effort could redeem a people from slavery to sin, but it is his alone, of whom it was said, 'Behold the Lamb of God. Behold him who taketh away the sin of the world' (John 1:29). The others saved a people that was not theirs but God's, not from sins but from their enemies.

XIII. 'Thou art our God,' says Isaiah, 'and we knew it not, the God of Israel, the Saviour' (Isaiah 45:15, LXX). Who do you think is more likely to say this, who say this more appropriately, the Jews, or the Gentiles? It was the Jews in fact who did not recognize Christ, for it is said, 'Israel hath not known me and my people hath not understood' (Isaiah 1:3). And again, 'the world was made by him, and the world knew him not. He came unto his own, and his own received him not' (John 1:10–11). Was it the Gentiles? It is clear that while the pagans were obsessed with idolatry they did not know Christ, but then they did not know the Father either: now however they do know the Father, nor do they know him except through Christ. You can see that the people who believe, whether they came from Jewish or Gentile origin, could in either case aptly say, 'Thou art our God, and we knew it not, the God of Israel, the Saviour.' The Gentiles, when they worshipped idols, did not know God: the Jews, denying Our Lord, did not know the Son of God. Both Jews and Gentiles may well say, therefore, of Christ, 'Thou art our God, and we knew it not.' The Gentiles who did not believe were as ignorant of God as the Jews who denied the Son of God.

Christ must therefore be believed, as the Truth has spoken, as the Godhead has proclaimed, as Christ himself has told us, for he is both Truth and Divinity. Why are you so insane as to insert a division between Christ and God? Why attempt to separate the Son of God from his own body? Why try to divide God? You are splitting up a unity, dismembering a whole. Believe the Word of God about God: you could have no better grounds for confessing the divinity of God, than if you profess with your lips what he says of himself, as the Godhead has taught you. Know, as the prophet has told you, that Our Lord is God: he who 'found out all the way of knowledge', who 'was seen upon earth and conversed with men' (Baruch 3:37–8). He brought the light of faith into the world, he showed us the light of salvation. Our Lord is God, and has shone upon us. Believe in him, therefore, love him, confess him. For as Scripture says, 'every knee would bow, of those that are in heaven, on earth, and under the earth; and that every tongue should confess that the Lord Jesus Christ is in the glory of God the Father' (Philippians 2:10–11). Whether you will or no, you cannot deny it; Our Lord Jesus Christ is in the glory of God the Father. This is the perfect force of a perfect faith, to confess that our Lord and God, Jesus Christ, is always in the glory of God the Father. Amen.

❖

✞ BOOK FIVE ✞

I. We said in the first book that the Nestorian heresy was a disciple
and imitator of the Pelagian, striving in every way to establish
that our Lord Jesus Christ, the Son of God, born of a virgin,
should be believed to be no more than a man. Only because he
had embarked on a virtuous life, did he obtain by his devout and
religious behaviour the reward of being associated with divine
majesty, because of the perfection of that life. The dignity of his
sacred origin was totally denied, and all that was left to him was
the fact that he was chosen for his merits. It follows from these
efforts to establish that doctrine, that Christ was sent as a man
among men, and assimilated to the mass of the human race, and
that by the practice of good works any other man could come
to merit the same reward as Christ did by his holy life. What a
pestilential opinion, how fatal! It detracts from the truth about
God, and makes false promises to men; in both cases the deception
is damnable, for it affronts God by the sacrilegious insult, and
lures men on in the hope of a false presumption. The very idea is
perverse and irreligious: it gives mortals something they do not
possess, but takes away from God what is his own. This recent
pernicious heresy that has sprung up, in its poisonous depravity,
has stirred up old ashes to revive them, and brought new fire into
the smouldering embers: for they assert that Our Lord Jesus Christ
was born as a mere man. What then must we look for; what is the
actual source of the error that results in this absurdity? It would
be pointless to investigate the outcome without investigating the
original root cause. So what is the principal error which now, just
as in the earlier heresy, attributes to man, what it takes away from
God? What a horror! In fact once we have seen what came before,

it would be almost sinful to investigate the consequences, for it could follow logically that it would not be wrong to go so far as to deny that God exists at all!

The new heresy, as we have frequently said, asserts that Our Lord Jesus Christ was born of the virgin as a mere man, and that Mary should therefore be called only *Christotokos*, not *Theotokos*, the Mother of Christ alone, not of God. To the former assertion is added the perverse and frivolous argument that no one gives birth to one older than herself. As if human reason could understand or explain the nativity of the only-begotten Son of God, which was foretold by the prophets and proclaimed through the ages! Do you imagine, O heretic whoever you be, that the Virgin Mary, whose child-bearing you revile, needed any merits of her own, to carry out what was done in her, so that you could use her human frailty as an objection to this great matter, this mighty work? If any of this had been done by human effort, then you may look for human reasoning, but since everything that happened was in fact the work of God, why talk about what is impossible for men, when you can see that it was done by God? I shall say more about this later. Now we must follow up what I had just begun to discuss, so that everyone may be aware that you are looking for your fires among the ashes of Pelagianism, and that you are arousing the ancient embers with your present bellowing.

II. You claim that Christ was born as a mere man. This is something which the wicked Pelagian heresy taught, as we showed in the first book, that Christ was born as no more than a man. Moreover you say that Jesus Christ, the Lord of all, should be called the image *Theodochos*, that is not God but the receiver of God. Thereby you think he should be honoured not for his own sake, as being God, but because he received God into himself. The Pelagian heresy also taught this, that Christ should not be honoured for himself, because he is God, but because he had earned the right to have God in himself through his good and holy actions. See how you are regurgitating that Pelagian poison, breathing the spirit of Pelagius! It follows that you do not appear to need condemnation, for you are already condemned, for in following the same error, you must fall under the same judgment. I will not mention the further point that you compare the Lord to a statue of the Emperor, for in that blasphemous pitch of sacrilege you have actually surpassed Pelagius in absurdity, though he had outclassed virtually everyone else in perversity.

III. So you say we should call Christ the image *theodochos*, and honour him not in himself as being God, but because he received God into himself. In this you are suggesting there is no difference between him and any of the saints, for every holy man has received God into himself. God dwelt in the Patriarchs; God spoke through the prophets, that we know well. We believe that not just the apostles and martyrs but every holy man of God, every servant of God, has the Spirit of God within himself, as it is written, 'you are the temple of the living God; as God saith: I will dwell in them' (II Corinthians 6:16). And again, 'Know you not that you are the temple of God and that the Spirit of God dwelleth in you?' (I Corinthians 3:16) All of therefore are *Theodochoi*, all of us are like unto Christ and equal with God according to you! Away with such impious abominations! Can he who created his own mother, the master of his servants, the God of heaven and earth, be assimilated to earthly frailty? His own goodness is turned into an insult, in that he who was pleased to dwell among men should be told that he is the same as a man.

IV. The difference between Christ and the saints is the difference between a dwelling and a dweller. A dwelling does not cause itself to be dwelt in: that is the work of the dweller, who is able to choose whether to build the dwelling, and whether to use it. When he wishes he can create a dwelling, and when he has made it he can decide to live in it. 'Do you seek a proof of Christ that speaketh in me?' asks the Apostle. 'Know you not your own selves, that Christ Jesus is in you, unless perhaps you be reprobates?' (II Corinthians 13:3, 5) And elsewhere, 'unto the inward man, that Christ may dwell by faith in your hearts' (Ephesians 3:16–17). Can you see the difference between your blasphemies and the teaching of the Apostles? You claim that God dwelt in Christ as in any man, St Paul bears witness that Christ himself dwelt among men. He is proved to be God because of what flesh and blood could not do, although you claim they could, and from that very fact you deny him to be God. For if you do not deny that he who dwells in a man could be God, it follows that we must believe the one whom we know did dwell among men to be God. All the patriarchs, all the prophets, all the apostles and martyrs, all saints of any kind, had God within them, all were made sons of God, all were *Theodochoi*, but differently, and according to a very diverse reason. All who believe in God are sons of God by adoption, but the Only-begotten alone is a son by nature. He was not begotten out of any matter by the Father, for all matter, all material things came to be through the only-begotten son of God. He was not begotten from nothing, for he is of the Father, not by childbirth, for there is nothing void or mutable about God; no, God the Father begat his only Son in a way that cannot be described or explained, in the unbegotten nature which was his. Thus the Son is sovereign, only-begotten and eternal, from the unbegotten eternal sovereign Father; he is the same person in the flesh as in the spirit; we believe in the same person in the flesh that we believe in majesty, for he was to be born in the flesh. He made no division or separation in himself, as if only part of him was born, and part not born, nor was there any divinity that came to him later that was not born in him from the Virgin. For as St Paul says, 'in Christ dwelleth all the fullness of the Godhead' (Colossians 2:9). The Godhead did not dwell in him at some times and not at other times, nor was it afterwards and not before. Otherwise we would fall into the impious Pelagian heresy, saying that God only dwelt in Christ after a certain time, only coming upon him when his life and behaviour had deserved that divine power could come to him. It is the part of men, ordinary men, not of God, to humble themselves before God and obey God as far as human frailty can, until they make themselves the dwelling place of God, and in their faithful piety are worthy to have God as their guest dwelling within them. To the extent that

someone is fitted for God's gift, to that extent does divine grace
reward him. If anyone is deemed worthy of God, he will be glad
in the presence of God, as Our Lord promised, 'If anyone love
me, he will keep my word. And my Father will love him; and we
will come to him and will make our abode with him' (John 14:23).
Of Christ the situation is very different, for in him 'dwelleth all
the fullness of the Godhead' (Colossians 2:9) He had the fullness
of divinity in himself in such a way that he could bestow of his
fullness to all others; He in whom dwelt the fullness of Godhead
dwells himself in each of the saints, in so far as he thinks them fit
for his dwelling; he gives to all of his fullness but remains himself
undiminished in that fullness. Even while he was in his body on
earth, he was in the souls of all his saints; he filled the heavens,
the earth and the seas, and the whole universe with his infinite
power and majesty, and yet was totally within himself, so that the
whole universe could not contain him. No matter how immense
and indescribable creation is, nothing is great enough or spacious
enough to contain the creator himself.

V. He is is of whom the prophet spoke, 'Only in thee is God; and
there is no God beside thee. Verily thou art our God, and we knew
it not, the God of Israel, the Saviour' (Isaiah 45:14–15, LXX). He
was 'seen upon earth and conversed with men' (Baruch 3:38), and
the Psalmist David spoke in his name, 'From my mother's womb
thou art my God' (Psalm 21/2:11). He shows us that the Man who
is Lord never existed apart from his unity with God, for while he
was in the very womb of the Virgin the fullness of godhead dwelt
in him. The same Psalmist says in another place, 'Truth is sprung
out of the earth; and justice hath looked down from heaven' (Psalm
84/5:12). Thus we may understand that the Son of God looked
down from heaven, that is to say he came to us, descended, and
was born as justice from the flesh of the Virgin, not a fictitious
body but a real one. For he himself is truth, as Truth himself bears
witness, 'I am the truth and the life' (John 14:6). As in the previous
books we have established the truth, that Our Lord Jesus Christ
was born of the Virgin as God, now and in the next book we learn

that he who was to be born of the Virgin was ever foretold to be God. Isaiah the prophet says, 'Cease ye therefore from the man, whose breath is in his nostrils, for in that matter he is reputed', or, to be more faithful to the Hebrew, 'for he is reputed high' (Isaiah 2:22). In the choice of the word 'cease' he expresses the force of a prohibition against troubling him with persecution. 'Cease ye therefore from the man, whose breath is in his nostrils, for he is reputed high.' Does not this single verse speak of the reception of a human body, and also of the truth that he is God? 'Cease ye therefore from the man, whose breath is in his nostrils, for he is reputed high.' Do you not see that he is clearly addressing those who persecuted the Lord, saying, 'Cease from the man', whom you are persecuting, for this man is God? Yes, he appears in the lowly form of a man, but he abides in the exalted state of divine splendour. Well does the prophet say, 'Cease ye therefore from the man, whose breath is in his nostrils', for he plainly shows his humanity by indicating the human body. The prophet is fearless and faithful, in affirming the truth of his humanity as steadily as that of his divinity, for the true and Catholic faith is to believe that Our Lord Jesus Christ had the true substance of a body, just as he had the perfect truth of divinity. Can you claim there is any ambiguity in his use of the word 'high' rather than 'God'? No, it is customary in Holy Scripture to use 'most high' for 'God', as in the psalm, 'The most High uttered his voice, the earth trembled' (Psalm 45/6:7), and, 'thou alone art the most High over all the earth' (Psalm 82/3:19). Isaiah also uses the word, 'the High and the Eminent that inhabiteth eternity' (Isaiah 57:15). We can understand from this quite clearly that just as in the latter text Isaiah uses 'the High' to mean God, with no other qualification, so in the former text he means God in the word 'the High'. It is clear, then, from that prophecy that the Word of God proclaims our Lord Jesus Christ to be both man and God: let us look now to see if the evidence of the New Testament will agree with that of the Old.

VI. 'That which was from the beginning', says St John, 'which we have heard, which we have seen with our eyes, which we have looked upon and our hands have handled, of the Word of life; for the life was manifested; and we have seen and do bear witness and declare unto you the life eternal, which was with the Father and hath appeared to us' (I John 1–2). See how the Old Testament is strengthened by the New, and the New Testament follows and strengthens what was foretold of old. Isaiah said, 'Cease from the man, whose breath is in his nostrils, for he is reputed High' (Isaiah 2:22), and John says, 'That which was from the beginning, which we have heard, which we have seen with our eyes, which we have looked upon and our hands have handled.' Isaiah says that he would be persecuted by the Jews as a man; St John says that as a man he was handled by human hands. Isaiah says that he whom he announces as a man was God most High; St John that he who was handled by men was God always in the beginning. Clearly they both declare Our Lord Jesus Christ to be both man and God, the same person who was always God became man afterwards, thus both man and God, for the man himself is God. 'That which was from the beginning, which we have heard, which we have seen with our eyes, which we have looked upon and our hands have handled, of the Word of life; for the life was manifested; and we have seen and do bear witness and declare unto you the life eternal, which was with the Father and hath appeared to us.' See how many indications, in such varied ways, does the beloved Apostle of God, so closely tied to him, use to teach us the mystery of the incarnation of God! To begin with, he gives evidence that he who always was, in the beginning, was seen in the flesh. Then, lest what he said about him being both seen and heard might not be enough to convince the doubters, he adds that he was handled, touched and pulled about by his own hands, and those of others. By showing how the flesh he assumed was real, he refutes the errors of the Marcionites and Manichees, for no one could imagine that people only saw a phantasm, when the apostle could bear witness that he had touched his body. He goes on to speak of the Word of life, and of life made manifest, which he himself had seen, was proclaiming, was affirming, so as to carry out his duty in faith, and to bring terror on the unbeliever, for as he claimed to preach, he also inferred the danger there is for those who refuse to listen. 'We bear witness and declare unto you the life eternal, which was with the Father and hath appeared to us.' He teaches us that what was always with the Father, has appeared to men; what was in the beginning always, has been seen by men; what was the Word of life without beginning, has been touched by human hands. How many different points he makes, how clear and distinct, to express the mystery of how flesh was united to God! No one has any excuse for speaking of either nature without mentioning both. Another Apostle said the same, 'Jesus Christ, yesterday and today; and the same for ever' (Hebrews 13:8). This agrees with what the previous text said, 'that which was from the beginning, which our hands have handled.' A spirit cannot of itself be felt by hands, but the Word made flesh could be touched in the humanity united with itself. It is the same Jesus, then, 'yesterday and today', the same who was before the beginning of the world, now in flesh; he same in the past as in the present, the same through the ages, for he is throughout all things as he was before all things. Our Lord Jesus Christ is all this.

VII. How then was he born before the world, he who has been born but lately? Simply because he who was recently born as man is the same person as God born before all things. All things that are said of God are said of Christ, for such is the unity between Christ and God that no one could possibly say, while speaking of Christ, that Christ is not God, nor while speaking of God that God is not Christ. Both natures are united in him, through the mystery of that sacred and majestic nativity, so that whatever there is of both man and God should all be made God. The Apostle Paul had his eyes opened to faith so that he saw the whole inexplicable secret of majesty in Christ; thus he spoke, inviting the people who acknowledged the goodness of God to attribute that goodness to his free grace. 'Giving thanks to God the Father, who hath made us worthy to be partakers of the lot of the saints in light; who hath delivered us from the power of darkness and hath translated us into the kingdom of the Son of his love; in whom we have redemption through his blood, the remission of sins; who is the image of the invisible God, the first-born of every creature. For in him were all things created in heaven and on earth, visible and invisible, whether thrones, or dominations, or principalities, or powers. All things were created by him and in him. And he is before all, and by him all things consist. And he is the head of the body, the Church; who is the beginning, the first-born from the dead, that in all things he may hold the primacy; because in him, it hath well pleased the Father that all fullness should dwell; and through him, to reconcile all things unto himself, making peace through the blood of his cross, both as to the things that are on earth and the things that are in heaven' (Colossians 1:12–20).

Does this need any further commentary? It is so clearly and fully set out that we find not only the essence of our faith, but its explanation as well. He bids us give thanks to the Father, and gives us the main reason for giving thanks, that he has made us worthy to share with the saints, has rescued us from the power of darkness and transferred us to the kingdom of the Son he loves. In Christ we have redemption, and the remission of sins; that Christ is the image of the invisible God, and the first-born of all creation. Everything was created in him, and through him; he was the one who made them, and he also controls and guides them. And then what? 'And he is the head of the body, the Church; who is the beginning, the first-born from the dead.' Scripture uses the word 'generation' for resurrection, for just as generation creates life, so the resurrection generates us to new life. The resurrection is therefore called the 'regeneration', in the words of Our Lord, 'Amen, I say to you that you who have followed me in the regeneration when the Son of man shall sit on the seat of his majesty, you also shall sit on twelve seats judging the twelve tribes of Israel' (Matthew 19:28). St Paul calls Christ the first-born from the dead, having already declared him to be the Son and image of the invisible God. The image of the invisible God is none other than the Only-begotten, the Word of God. How then is he said to have been raised from the dead, he who is called the image and the Word of God invisible? What does St Paul say next? 'That in all things he may hold the primacy; because in him, it hath well pleased the Father that all fullness should dwell; and through him, to reconcile all things unto himself, making peace through the blood of his cross, both as to the things that are on earth and the things that are in heaven.'

Does the Creator of the whole universe stand in need of any primacy; does he who made them need primacy over the things which he himself has made? What can we say of the Word? In him, who was the first-born of the dead, it pleased the Father that all fullness should dwell? He was the only-begotten Son of God, the Word of God before the beginning of all things; he possessed the invisible Father within himself, and contained in himself all fullness beforehand—can we say now that he himself was all fullness? And what does St Paul say next? 'Making peace through the blood of his cross, both as to the things that are on earth and the things that are in heaven.' He makes it clear about whom he is speaking, by naming him the first-born from the dead. Were all things reconciled and pacified by the blood of the Word, or of the Spirit? No indeed. No form of suffering could affect an impassible nature; no blood could be shed to any avail save that of a man; no one could die except a man. Yet he who in the sequel is described as dead, was before announced as the image of the invisible God. Why should this be? Because the apostles took every precaution to avoid giving the impression of any division in Christ; otherwise the Son of God, united with the Son of Man, might be misinterpreted as having two persons, so that evil and depraved teachers would make him who is united in himself become twofold in our eyes. Therefore the Apostle's teaching leads beautifully from the only-begotten Son of God to the Son of Man who is united to the Son of God; just as it happened in reality, so the course of his teaching follows. He links everything and makes a bridge, as it were, in an unbreakable connection, so that with no division or separation, the one of whom you read in the beginning of the world you will find at the end of time. You cannot be diverted by any unlawful division into thinking that there was one Son of God in the flesh and another in the spirit. The authority of the apostle has united

God and man in the mystery of his bodily nativity, so that he can reveal to you that he who reconciles all things on the cross is the same person as the one he had proclaimed as the image of the invisible God before the creation of the world.

VIII.　Now what we have heard spoken by the Apostle is the actual teaching of Our Lord. What St Paul wrote to the first Christians is the same as what Jesus himself said of himself to the Jews in the Gospel: 'Now you seek to kill me, a man who have spoken the truth to you, which I have heard of God. For I came not of myself, but he sent me' (John 8:40, 42). Here he speaks of himself as both God and man. He is a man, for he calls himself a man, he is God, for he confirms that he was sent. He must have been with the one from whom he came; he came from the one from whom he says he was sent. Hence when the Jews said to him, 'Thou art not fifty years old; and hast thou seen Abraham?' he responded in words that were fitting to his eternal majesty, 'Amen, amen, I say to you, before Abraham was made, I AM' (John 8:57–8). Now, I ask you, who do you think was speaking? Christ, without a doubt. And how could he who had been born at a recent period, say that he is before Abraham? Only thus: through the Word of God to whom he was totally united, so that all should understand how close is the union between Christ and God, so that whatever God says in Christ he could claim totally for himself, through that divine unity. Fully conscious of his eternity, Jesus responded, in the body, to the Jews with the words which he had once spoken to Moses in the spirit. Here he says, 'before Abraham was made, I AM', but to Moses he said, 'I AM WHO AM' (Exodus 3:14). With words of splendid appropriateness he defines the eternity of his divine nature, for there is nothing you can say of God more significant than that he always is. That being has neither beginning in the past nor ending in the future. He is thus clearly telling us of his nature as the eternal God, which is aptly linked to eternity. Our Lord Jesus Christ himself, when speaking about Abraham, uses a variety of expression, for he says, 'before Abraham was made, I AM'. Of Abraham he says 'before he was made', but of himself

'I AM'. Being made belongs in time; simple Being, in eternity. The being made he attributes to brief human life; the I AM to his own nature. Both of these attributes belong to Christ, for by the mystery of his union of man and God, he can say he always was in him who always is.

IX. The apostle wanted to demonstrate this clearly to everyone, so he said, 'Jesus, having saved the people out of the land of Egypt, did afterwards destroy them that believed not' (Jude 5). In another text, 'neither let us tempt Christ, as some of them tempted and perished by the serpents' (I Corinthians 10:9). The chief of the Apostles, Peter, said, 'Now therefore, why tempt you God to put a yoke upon the necks of the disciples which neither our fathers nor we have been able to bear? But by the grace of the Lord Jesus Christ, we believe to be saved, in like manner as they also' (Acts 15:10–11). We know that it was none other than God who freed the people of God from Egypt, and led them dryshod through the vast expanse of the waters, and preserved them in the immense emptiness of the desert, for it is written, 'The Lord alone was his leader: and there was no strange god with him' (Deuteronomy 32: 12). So how can the Apostles in all those clear passages tell us that it was by Jesus that the people of the Jews were liberated from Egypt, and that it was Christ who was provoked in the desert by the Jews, in that text, 'neither let us tempt Christ, as some of them tempted and perished by the serpents.' Moreover the blessed Apostle Peter proclaims that it was by the grace of Our Lord Jesus Christ that all the holy men who lived under the old covenant were saved. So get out of that if you can, any of you who are so rabid and blasphemous as to assert that there is no real difference between Adam and Christ, who deny that he was God even after he was born of the Virgin: show us whether you can persuade us that he was not God before he was born! See: the Apostle declares that the people were liberated from the land of Egypt by Jesus, that Christ was tempted in the desert by those who were unfaithful, that our ancestors, that is the patriarchs and prophets, were saved by the grace of Our Lord Jesus Christ: deny that if you can!

I will not be surprised if you do deny it, contradicting the text we all read, refusing what we all believe. But be aware that Christ did already lead the people out of Egypt in God; Christ was provoked by the trying people, in God; in God, Christ saved all the just by the free grace he gave. This is because the mystery of the union means that God is in Christ and Christ in God, so that whatever God did was done by Christ, whatever Christ did later, is said to be the work of God. Therefore the Psalmist says, 'there shall be no new god in thee; neither shalt thou adore a strange god' (Psalm 80/81:10). In this way, and with this meaning, he foretold how the Apostle would say that Christ was the one who brought the people of Israel out of Egypt, knowing that he who was born as man of the Virgin had always been in God because of the mystery of the unity. Otherwise one would have to believe as the heretics do that Christ is not God, or contradict the Psalmist by believing in a new god. The Catholic people of God could never contradict a prophet or agree with a heretic! Could the people of the blessing fall under the curse of having put their hope in a mere man? If you do assert that Our Lord Jesus Christ was born as a mere man, you would have to fall under two curses, whether you believe in him or not. If you do put your trust in him, then 'cursed be the man that trusteth in man' (Jeremiah 17:5). If you do not, then you will be cursed just the same, for even if you do not trust in man, you will have totally denied God.

X. This is what the Lord revealed to that beloved disciple of God, St John, when he prophesied, speaking of the very one who was speaking through him, 'Every spirit which confesseth that Jesus Christ is come in the flesh is of God; and every spirit that dissolveth Jesus is not of God; and this is Antichrist, of whom you have heard that he cometh; and he is now already in the world' (I John 4:2–3). How marvellous is the unparalleled love of God! Like a sage physician he foretells in advance the ills that are to come on the Church! When he foretold the disease, he foretold also the cure, so that anyone who recognizes the onset of the infection can begin at once to take steps to avoid what he knows is approaching. Hence St John says, 'every spirit that dissolveth Jesus is not of God; and this is Antichrist.' Do you recognize him, O heretic? Do you recognize that he is specifically talking about you? There is no one who dissolves Jesus other than the one who does not confess that he is God. The whole creed of the Church, all her worship, is to acclaim Jesus as true God, so how could anyone do more to dissolve his honour and worship than by denying what it is in him that we worship? Beware, I beseech you, beware lest anyone be able to call you Antichrist! Do you think I am reviling you or cursing? I am not choosing my own words, for see what the Evangelist says, 'every spirit that dissolveth Jesus is not of God; and this is Antichrist.' No one could call you Antichrist unless you dissolve Jesus and deny God. If you do deny him, why complain if anyone call you Antichrist? You yourself have said it of yourself, just by denying him. Do you believe it? Tell me, when Jesus was born of the Virgin, do you think he was a man, or God? If he is only God, you are dissolving Jesus, by denying that man was united with God in him. If he is only man, you dissolve him just as much, if you blasphemously assert that it was a mere man who was born.

Could it be that you imagine that you are not dissolving Jesus, in denying him to have been God, while you are certainly dissolving him by denying that the man who was born was with God. Do you want examples to make this clear? See them, on both sides: Manichaeus is outside the Church, and he asserted that Jesus was only God; so is Ebion, who claimed he was but man. Both of them dissolved Jesus and denied him, one by saying he was only a man, the other saying he was only God. They said opposite things, but were equally wrong in what they said. Though if there can be any gradation in malice, your blasphemy is the worse, in saying he is only a man, than the other which says he is only God, for while both are wrong, it is worse to deprive the Lord of his divine nature than of his human. The Catholic faith, which is the only true one, is to believe that Our Lord Jesus Christ is as much man as God, as much God as man. 'Every spirit that dissolveth Jesus is not of God.' To dissolve him is this, to attempt to break apart

what is united in Jesus, to separate out what is one entity. What is
it that is united and one in Jesus? His humanity and his divinity.
Therefore he who dissolveth Jesus is the one who separates and
disjoins these two natures. [If you do not disrupt and separate, you
do not dissolve; if you separate and disrupt, you are dissolving.]

XI. Now if any man does fall into this insane blasphemy, he
is addressed and rebuked by Our Lord Jesus himself, when he
speaks on his own behalf to the Pharisees in the Gospel, 'What
God hath joined together, let not man put asunder' (Matthew
19:6). Of course, those words of God do seem to be the reply
to another question, but God is so profound that he speaks of
spiritual matters more than of fleshly ones, and while he wanted
them to understand those words in their obvious context, he even
more wanted them to understand them about his own nature.
The Jews already held your opinion, that Jesus was merely a man
without God, so when they asked him about the law of marriage,
he taught them not only about that but about this as well. They
asked him about a lesser matter, he told them of a greater, when
he said, 'What God hath joined together, let not man put asunder.'
Do not separate, he means, what God has put together in me; let
impious men not disjoin what the majesty of God united in me.
    If you want to hear this more clearly, hear what St Paul says
when he speaks of the same matters that Our Saviour was then
teaching. He was sent by God as a teacher, to explain what God
had taught in an obscure way so that weak human understanding
could grasp it. When St Paul speaks about earthly marriage, which
is what Our Lord had been asked about in the gospel, he quotes
the same Old Testament text that Our Lord had used, so that his
hearers should understand that he was explaining the same matter,
using the same texts. Lest any part of the matter should be missed,
he mentions in addition the earthly marriage of a man and a
woman, and exhorts them to mutual affection, saying, 'Husbands,
love your wives, as Christ also loved the Church.' Then he goes on,
'So also ought men to love their wives as their own bodies. He that
loveth his wife loveth himself. For no man ever hated his own flesh,

but nourisheth and cherisheth it, as also Christ doth the Church; because we are members of his body' (Ephesians 5:25, 28–9). See how he associates the names of Christ and the Church with the mention of a husband and wife: thus he leads us on from hearing of fleshly matters to understanding spiritual ones. And after saying all this, he concludes with the text which Our Lord used in the Gospel, saying, 'For this cause shall a man leave his father and mother; and shall cleave to his wife; and they shall be two in one flesh' (Ephesians 5:31, cf. Matthew 19:5; cf. Genesis 2:24). After that he continues as if making a loud proclamation, 'This is a great sacrament.' He eliminates any possibility of fleshly understanding, in saying that it is a sacrament or mystery of divinity. And what then follows? 'But I speak in Christ and in the church' (Ephesians 5:32). When he had said this is a great sacrament, he did not say 'and this is the explanation of the mystery.' What did he say? 'I speak in Christ and in the church.' That is to say, it is indeed a great mystery, and I am applying it to Christ and the Church. Since not all may yet be able to understand, they may at least understand this; the lesser point is not alien or contradictory to the greater, for both relate to Christ, so that those who are incapable of profound truth may at least be able to grasp something easier. Then when their understanding begins to become more acute they may attain to deeper matters, so that their grasp of the simpler point may become the path to greater profundity.

XII. Now what is this great mystery or sacrament which is indicated by naming a man and wife? Let us ask St Paul himself, who in another place uses the very same words to teach the same doctrine: 'And evidently great is the mystery of godliness, which was manifested in the flesh, was justified in the spirit, appeared unto angels, hath been preached unto the Gentiles, is believed in the world, is taken up in glory' (I Timothy 3:16). So what is the great mystery which was manifested in the flesh? God, surely, born of the flesh, God visible in a body, for just as he was openly manifested in the flesh, so was he openly assumed into glory. This is the great mystery, of which he said, 'For this cause shall a man leave his father and mother; and shall cleave to his wife; and they shall be two in one flesh.' The two who were in one flesh are God and the human soul. In one human flesh, united to God, is both the Godhead and a human soul, as the Lord himself tells us, 'No man taketh my soul away from me; but I lay it down of myself. And I have power to lay it down; and I have power to take it up again' (John 10:18). Three things, now, you can see in one: God, the flesh, the soul. It is God who speaks, the flesh in which he speaks, the soul of which he speaks. That is the man of whom the prophet says, 'No brother can redeem, man shall redeem' (Ps. 48/9:8, LXX). He is the man who, as it is said, 'ascended up where he was before' (John 6:63), and of whom we read, 'No man hath ascended into heaven, but he that descended from heaven, the Son of man who is in heaven' (John 3:13). Therefore I say, 'shall a man leave his father and mother'; namely God from whom he was born, and that Jerusalem which is mother of us all, 'and shall cleave to' human flesh, as if to 'his wife'. He says explicitly of the Father, that a man shall leave his own father; of the mother he does not say 'his own', but just says 'mother', for she is not so much his mother as that of all believers, that is all of us. He adds then 'to his wife', for just as a man and his wife are one body, so the divine majesty and human flesh are united, and the two become one, God and the soul in one flesh. The flesh contained God dwelling in itself, and also the human soul which dwelt there with God. This is the great sacrament or mystery which the admiring Apostle calls us to consider, as does God's own invitation. It is not inappropriate to Christ and the Church, for St Paul himself says, 'I speak in Christ and in the Church.' The flesh of the Church is the flesh of Christ, and in the flesh of Christ is God, and the human soul. Thus what is true of Christ is true of the Church, and the mystery which is believed of the flesh of Christ is also contained by faith in the Church.

XIII. This mystery, then, which was manifested in the flesh, has appeared in the world, has been preached to the Gentiles, was foreseen in the spirit by many of the saints of old, and indeed they longed to see it in the flesh. 'Amen, I say to you,' says the Lord, 'many prophets and just men have desired to see the things that you see and have not seen them, and to hear the things that you hear, and have not heard them' (Matthew 13:17). Isaiah the prophet said, therefore, 'O that thou wouldst rend the heavens and wouldst come down' (Isaiah 64:1). David also sang, 'Lord, bow down thy heavens and descend' (Psalm 143:5), and Moses said, 'Show thyself unto me, that clearly I may know thee' (Exodus 33:13, LXX). No one approached God closer than Moses, for he received the Law, and God spoke to him from the cloud, in the very presence of the majesty. So how, if no one saw God more closely than he, how can he ask him to be shown more clearly, as he says, 'Show thyself unto me, that clearly I may know thee.' Surely he was praying that would happen to him which the Apostle declares has actually happened, using the same words, namely that the Lord be manifested clearly in the flesh, appear openly to the world, be openly assumed into glory; thus the saints saw with their fleshly eyes all these things which they had foreseen in their spiritual sight.

XIV. Now if it were true what the heretics say, that God was to come in Our Lord Jesus Christ as if into a statue or instrument, in other words that he was to live in him as in any man, and speak as he does through any man, rather than himself being the person he inhabits so that God himself speaks of himself in his own body—if that were true, then he would have lived in the saints and spoken through the saints in the same way. Thus he would have dwelt and spoken in those very saints of whom I spoke earlier, who prayed for his coming. So why should they have asked for something they already had, why look for something they had already received? Why should they desire to see with their eyes what they possessed in their hearts, especially since it is better to possess something within oneself than to see it outside? If God were merely going to live in Christ as he does in every saint, why did all those saints desire to see Christ rather than themselves? If what they were to see in the Lord Jesus was the same as they had in themselves, why did they not think it better to possess it in themselves instead of seeing it in another? No, you are wrong, and miserably so, 'understanding neither the things they say, nor whereof they affirm' (I Timothy 1:7)! All the prophets, all the saints of old, received from God only a share in the divine Spirit, in accordance with their capacity, but in Christ there dwelt, and yet 'dwelleth, all the fullness of the Godhead corporeally' (Colossians 2:9). They are far from his fullness, though they receive something from his fullness (cf. John 1:16), for their fulfilment is a gift from Christ. They were all empty, were it not that he is the fullness of all.

XV.　This is what all the ancient saints longed for, what they prayed for, what they desired to see with their eyes as they perceived it in mind and soul: thus the prophet Isaiah cried out, 'O that thou wouldst rend the heavens and wouldst come down' (Isaiah 64:1). Thus Habacuc proclaimed the same truth that Isaiah longed for, 'When the years approach thou shalt make it known: in the coming of the ages thou shalt manifest it: God will come from Theman' (or 'from the South') (Habacuc 3:2–3, VL). David also says, 'God shall come manifestly' (Psalm 49/50:3), and 'Thou that sitteth upon the cherubims; shine forth' (Psalm 79/80:2). Some announced the coming of him who was to save the world; others begged for it. Some, who were different in appearance but equal in affection, had some understanding of what they were asking for, that God should dwell in God; that while remaining in the form of God, and in his bosom, he should empty himself, assuming the form of a slave, subjecting himself even to the extent of accepting all the bitterness and reproach of his passion; that he should be punished for doing good, and should receive death at the hands of those for whom he was to die, how unbearable, how unworthy! The saints all understood something of this, had some grasp of it I tell you, though none of them understood it all, yet with one accord and common consent they begged for the coming of God. They knew that hope for all of them consisted in this, that this comprised the salvation of all, for no one could loose their bonds save one who was immune from bondage; no one could redeem sinners save one who was free from sin; no one could liberate anyone from anything unless he himself were free from whatever the other was to be liberated from. Thus since death came upon all men, all were in need of life; as in Adam all die, so in Christ are all made alive. There were many holy men, many chosen ones, many who were close to God, but none of them could be saved by themselves, for they were saved only by the coming of the Lord and his redemption.

❖

✝ Book Six ✝

I. We read in the Gospel how the Lord bade them bring five loaves, and a vast crowd of the people of God were fed (John 6). How this was done cannot be explained in words, or understood in thought, or perceived by the senses. The effect of divine power is so great, and so incomprehensible, that even though we are internally aware of what has been done, we are incapable of understanding the means by which it was done. Who, to begin with, can understand how such a small number of loaves would suffice even to be divided and apportioned among so many, not to mention enough to satisfy them all, for there were as many thousand people as there were loaves, and more meals required than there could be crumbs from so few loaves? But from the word of the Lord came forth such an abundance of matter. His work grew in the performing. What was seen was small, but what was achieved was incomprehensible. There is no scope here for human conjecture, estimation or reasoning. The only thing that the minds of the faithful and wise may understand in this matter is that however great the works of God are, and however incomprehensible, no matter if the senses cannot grasp them, we should realise that nothing is impossible for God. But we shall say more later about these actions of divine power that are beyond description, for our subject itself demands it, since it relates to the ineffable miracle of Christ's sacred birth.

II. But since we have mentioned the five loaves, I do not think it incongruous to compare them to the five books which we have already perused. They are alike in number, and not dissimilar in nature. Those loaves were of barley, and these books can be said to be of barley, with regards to our understanding, for although they are rich with sacred texts, they conceal their nourishment behind a harsh exterior. Another way in which they resemble each other is that barley loaves are poor in appearance, but became rich through being blessed, and my books are insignificant with regard to my ability, but precious because of the sacred things mixed in with them. My choice of words makes them look as rough as barley, but inside they taste of the bread of life because of the word of God they contain. Moreover through the gift of divine grace they may provide the food of salvation to innumerable people; just as those loaves gave bodily strength to those who ate them, so these books confer spiritual nourishment on those who read them. The Lord is powerful, and this is his gift to us, that by these books he prevents those who are nourished from falling away, just as by that food he prevented those who ate from fainting on the way.

A vast throng, therefore, of the people of God were fed with a small mouthful which was of great benefit; we read moreover that two fishes were added to the five loaves, so it is reasonable, if we want to provide adequate spiritual nourishment for all those people who follow God, that we should add two more books, like two fishes, to the five books which are like the loaves. We beseech you, therefore, O Lord, asking you to look upon the efforts we make in your service, and to grant that our labour will have a real effect. Since we are trying to equal the number of loaves and fishes with the number of our books, out of piety and devotion, grant now to these books the blessing you gave then. You can number our poor writings by that scriptural number, so fulfil the number of the outcome in the Gospel, and grant that these may bring holy and saving nourishment to all the people of your Church, of whatever age or sex. And if there be any who have been puffed up by the deadly breath of that poisonous serpent, their hearts and minds corrupted, and a lethal virus circulating in their veins, grant them all the vigour of sound understanding, grant them a truly healthy faith, so that through these writings of ours you can bestow on them all the gift of a healing remedy. Just as you made holy that food in the Gospel, so that you could strengthen their bodies through eating it, grant that those who are now weak may find healing in this work.

III. Now I think I have made an ample reply to the heretic who denies God in everything I have written already, using the authority of sacred texts. Let us turn to the faith and meaning expressed in the Creed of Antioch. The heretic was baptized with that creed, and reborn, so we ought to refute him with what he himself has professed, to defeat him with his own weapons, so to speak. Now he has been overcome with sacred scripture, it follows next that he should be defeated on his own evidence. There will be no need to bring any further argument against him, once he has clearly convicted himself.

The text of the Creed of Antioch is this: *I believe in one only true God, the Father almighty, creator of all things created, visible and invisible; and in Our Lord Jesus Christ, his only begotten Son, the first-born of all creation, who was born of him before all ages, and was not made; true God from true God, consubstantial with the Father; through him the ages were assembled, and all things made; he came for our sake and was born of the Virgin Mary, he was crucified under Pontius Pilate and was buried; on the third day he rose according to the Scriptures, and ascended to heaven; he will come again to judge the living and the dead* ... And so on.

Now in the Creed, which recounts the faith of all the Churches, I would like to ask you which authority you prefer to follow, that of man or God? I do not want to treat you severely or strictly, as to give you the option of choosing simply one thing or the other, while I observe one and deny the other: no, I will give you both, I will grant you both. What do I mean, give? No, I will compel you to choose both, willing or no; if you are willing to recognize that both are in the Creed, you will do so willingly; if you do not want to recognize it, you shall be made to. As you know the Creed is called a 'symbol', meaning that it is a collation. The Greek word *symbolon* is *collatio* in Latin. It is a collation, therefore, because you can find the whole Catholic faith in it, collected by the Lord's Apostles. Everything that is found in the vast body of all the sacred writings, is collected in perfect brevity into the Creed. St Paul says, 'He shall finish his word and cut it short in justice; because a short word shall the Lord make upon the earth' (Romans 9:28, quoting Isaiah 10:23). The short word that the Lord made is the faith of the two Testaments collected into a few words, the meaning of all the Scriptures encapsulated briefly, for the Lord set forth his own meaning in his own words, and perfected the force of the whole law in a brief text that expressed all. As a kindly father, he took into consideration both the negligence of some of his sons, and their ignorance, so that no matter how simple and inexperienced they might be, their minds should not find it difficult to understand what can easily be committed to memory.

IV. See now how God's authority is expressed in the Creed, 'because a short word shall the Lord make upon the earth'. But you complain, maybe, that the Creed is only a human text? Certainly, God wrote it through human means. Just as the whole huge collection of sacred writings was created through the means of the patriarchs and prophets, so God established the Creed through his apostles and bishops. Everything that he expounded in broad and ample abundance through his prophets in the Scriptures, is here summed up into a brief text by his bishops. There is nothing missing from the Creed, for the Apostles of God grounded it on the divine Scriptures, so that it contains within itself all authority, both that of men and of God. Although it was made by men, it must be attributed to God, for we believe that it pertains not so much to those through whom it was made as to him who made it.

The Creed says, therefore, *I believe in one only true God, the Father almighty, creator of all things created, visible and invisible; and in Our Lord Jesus Christ, his only begotten Son, the first-born of all creation, who was born of him before all ages, and was not made; true God from true God, consubstantial with the Father; through him the ages were assembled, and all things made; he came for our sake and was born of the Virgin Mary, he was crucified under Pontius Pilate and was buried; on the third day he rose according to the Scriptures, and ascended to heaven; he will come again to judge the living and the dead . . .* And so on.

V. Now, had you been a follower of the Arian or Sabellian heresy, I would not be able to cite your own creed against you, though I could still refute you on the authority of sacred scripture, I could convince you by the words of the Law itself, and overcome you at last with the truth of the creed which is accepted by the whole world. I could tell you that, even if you were bereft of understanding and sense, you should at least follow the consensus of the whole human race and should not take more account of the perversity of a few eccentrics than of the faith of all the churches. That faith was grounded by Christ, and passed on by the Apostles, so that we should consider it to be no less than the authoritative voice of God, which expresses the words and meaning of God. And if I were to act thus towards you, what could you say? What answer could you give? Surely only this: you would say that you were not brought up or educated in this way, you learnt something different from your parents, from your teachers and authorities. You did not learn the Catholic teaching in those chapels where your fathers taught, nor in the assemblies of your religion, and the text and meaning of the creed which was given to you contained something different. That was the belief in which you were baptized and reborn. You would assert that you were holding to what you had received, and lived by that in which you were reborn. And in saying that, would you not be using a very effective shield against the faith? Truly in any business, no matter how wrong, it would not be a futile defence, would not be called unreasonable as a source of error, as long as that error was not accompanied by stubbornness. If you hold onto what you were taught as a child, it would be more difficult to correct your current beliefs than to condemn those former ones adequately.

But in fact you were born in a Catholic city, instructed in the Catholic faith, and reborn in Catholic baptism—how can I deal with you as I would with an Arian or a Sabellian? Would that you were! I would grieve less over one badly brought up than one fallen away from a good upbringing; less over faith never possessed than faith lost, less over an established heretic than a new apostate. You would do less harm, cause less infection to the whole Church, you would be less bitter in the grief you would cause, less perilous as an example, had you been a popular ranter attacking the Church rather than a bishop presiding over it! Therefore, as I have said, had you been a disciple and promoter of the Arian, Sabellian or any other heresy, you would be esteemed as one who followed your parents' example, your teachers' instruction, your people's company, your own formula of belief. I am not asking anything unjust or burdensome, O heretic. Since you were educated as a Catholic, do what you might have done had you been educated in error: hold firm to what your parents taught you, hold firm to the faith of the Church, hold firm to the truth of the Creed, hold firm to the salvation of your baptism! What sort of an extraordinary monster are you? Do for yourself what others do for their own errors.

But we have gone far enough into the deep, in the quest for the familiar city we love we have followed the urgings of our grief as if it were a favouring wind: we have been so eager for the voyage that we have exceeded a reasonable rate of progress.

VI.   Now, O heretic, the Creed whose text we have already quoted, expresses the belief of all the Churches, for the faith of all is one, but it is in particular the formula of the city and church of Antioch, in other words that in which you were brought up, instructed and reborn. It was the profession of this formula of faith that led you to the font of life, to your regeneration for salvation, to the grace of the Eucharist and Communion with the Lord. And more than that—how grievous and doleful it is to recount! More than that: it led you to the office of the ministry, to the heights of the presbyterate, to the dignity of the episcopate. Do you consider this something trivial or irrelevant in your miserable folly? Do you not see what you have done? Into what a pit you have fallen? If you lose the formula of your faith, you have lost everything that you have been, for the sacraments of your high priesthood and your very salvation depend on the truth of the Creed. Do you imagine you can deny that? You would be denying your very self. But maybe you do not realize that you would be denying yourself: so let us look at the text of the Creed, so that if you still say what you did then, we shall not argue, but if you are saying things quite different and contrary, you will not need me to refute you, for you will have condemned yourself. If you assert something different from what is in the Creed, other than what you yourself first professed, it follows that you cannot blame anyone but yourself for condemning you, and you will see that everyone's opinion of you is the same as your own.

The Creed goes, *I believe in one only true God, the Father almighty, creator of all things created, visible and invisible; and in Our Lord Jesus Christ, his only begotten Son, the first-born of all creation, who was born of him before all ages, and was not made.* Here you must begin by answering, do you confess this about Jesus Christ, the Son of God, or do you not? If you confess it, everything is all right. But if not, how can you deny what you did confess before? Choose which you would rather, for you must choose one of the two: either let your own profession of faith remain as it was, and that is enough to set you free, or deny it, and that will condemn you. *I believe*, you said in the Creed, *in Our Lord Jesus Christ, his only begotten Son, the first-born of all creation.* If Our Lord Jesus Christ is the only-begotten and first-born of all creation, he is undoubtedly, on your own admission, God. For there is no other only-begotten first-born of all creation except the only-begotten Son of God. As he was the first-born of all creation, so he is God, the creator of all. How can you claim he was born of the Virgin as a mere man, when you have confessed that he was God before the ages? And the Creed goes on, *who was born of the Father before all ages, and was not made.* This is the Creed that you pronounced, you said this in the Creed, that Jesus Christ was born of God the Father before the ages, and was not made. Does the Creed say any of the fantasies that you are now promulgating? Did you yourself then talk of them? Where is that talk of 'statues' or 'instruments' of yours? They cannot be anyone's but your own. Where do you find that Our Lord Jesus Christ is like a statue, not worshipped as God but only as the image of God? Whence your blasphemy that makes the Lord's majesty a musical instrument, respected not for its own sake, but for the sake of the one who blows and sounds through it? You said in the Creed that Our Lord Jesus Christ was born of God the Father before the ages, and was not made, which can only mean that he was the only-begotten Son of God, in that his nativity did not mean that he was created, for he is said only to be born, not made. It would be contrary to the truth, and the dignity of the truth, to imagine the maker of all to be made, as if he, the author of all that comes to be did himself come to be, just as all things that have come to be came to be through him. He is said to be born, not made, for his nativity is unique, he was not made like all else. Since he is God, born from God, he must of necessity possess the divinity of the one who is begotten, and the whole greatness of the one who begot him.

VII. The Creed continues, *true God from true God, consubstantial with the Father; through him the ages were assembled, and all things made.* When you have said all that, remember you said it about the Lord Jesus Christ. That is what you find in the Creed, that you believe in the Lord Jesus Christ, the only-begotten Son of God, and the first-born of all creation. After that comes, *true God from true God, consubstantial with the Father, through whom the ages were assembled.* So how can the same person be God and not God, the same person be both God and a statue, God and an instrument? It does not make sense, O heretic, it is not consistent to call him God when you want to, and to imagine he is not real when you want to. You said in the Creed that he is true God—now you say he is a mere man! How can this fit together, how can this be so, that he who is all strength can be mere weakness, he who is all majesty, be simple mortality? These things cannot all be true of one and the same Lord, to divide him into what we worship and what we despise, giving honour to the part you choose, and choosing to disdain another. You said in the Creed, when you received the sacrament of true salvation, that Our Lord Jesus Christ is true God from true God, consubstantial with the Father, the creator of the ages, the maker of all. So where are, you, alas, where are you as you once were? Where is that faith, that confession? You have withdrawn into something strange and mysterious. What idiotic folly has caused you to fall thus? You have transformed the God of all power and might into a vain creature, a senseless imagination; your faith has deteriorated with time, age and your priesthood! As an old man you have become worse than when you were a child, as a veteran inferior to a novice, as a bishop lower than a catechumen; you did not begin to be a disciple until after you had been made a master.

VIII. But let us look at the words that follow. The Creed says, *the Lord Jesus Christ, true God from true God, consubstantial with the Father; through him the ages were assembled, and all things made;* and immediately after that come the words, *he came for our sake and was born of the Virgin Mary.* The same person, then, who was true God, who was consubstantial with the Father, the creator of the ages and maker of all things, that same person, I say, came into the world, and was born of the Virgin Mary. As St Paul the Apostle tells us, 'when the fullness of time was come, God sent his Son, made of a woman, made under the law' (Galatians 4:4). See how Holy Scripture agrees with the teaching contained in the Creed! The Apostle proclaims that the Son of God was sent by the Father, the Creed confirms that he came. It follows, then, that our faith should accept that he came, for the Apostle teaches us that he was sent.

St Paul continues, 'made of a woman', while the Creed says he was procreated through Mary. See how the Scripture is cited in the Creed, and the Creed gives its own evidence that it derives from that Scripture. The Apostle says, truly, 'made of a woman', using 'made' for 'born', which is common in the sacred writings, which use 'made' for 'born', as in, 'instead of thy fathers, sons are made to thee' (Psalm 44:17, LXX), and also, 'before Abraham was made, I AM' (John 8:58). In the latter he obviously means, before he was born, I am, for he uses the word 'made' to signify his birth, since anything that does not have necessary existence comes under the term 'made'.

He came for our sake, it continues, *and was born of the Virgin Mary.* If it were a mere man who was born of the Virgin Mary, how could he be said to have come? He could not have come, did he not already have existence so that he could come. For how could one who had not yet received existence have the ability to come? You can see therefore, how he is already described as coming by using the word 'coming', for he would have had no power to do so, had he not possessed the ability to come from the very fact of his existence. The man did not exist at all before his conception, so he did not have the ability to come. But we know for sure that God came, and he had the potentiality both to be and to come. He came, therefore, because he already existed: because he was always able to come means that he existed always.

IX. But why are we arguing about words, when the reality is so clear? Why are we looking for proof of the matter in the text of the Creed, when the facts speak for themselves? Let us look again at the profession of the Creed because it is your own; your own as much as the creed's, for you made it your own when you professed it. Be aware that you are not only disagreeing with the Creed but with yourself. *I believe*, says the Creed, *in one only true God, the Father almighty, creator of all things created, visible and invisible; and in the Lord Jesus Christ, his only begotten Son, the first-born of all creation, who was born of him before all ages, and was not made; true God from true God, consubstantial with the Father; through him the ages were assembled, and all things made; he came for our sake and was born of the Virgin Mary.* For our sake, it says, Our Lord Jesus Christ came and was born of the Virgin Mary, *crucified under Pontius Pilate and was buried; and rose, according to the Scriptures.* The Churches are not ashamed to confess this, the Apostles unashamed to proclaim it. It is you, you alone, whose every word is a scandal; before you denied nothing but now you deny it all, that God was born, that God suffered, that God rose again. What next? Where will you go now? What can you do, or feel or say? What will you regurgitate next? As the proverb goes, 'No sane man would say it, nor would Orestes so swear if he were sane' (A. Persius Flaccus, *Satura* III, 118). But what are your words? You said, 'What does it mean to say that the Son of God was born of the *Christotokos*? Imagine if we were to say, "I believe in God the Word, the Son of God, the only-begotten one born of the Father, consubstantial with the Father, who descended and was buried"—would not the very hearing of it wound our ears—that God could be dead!' And again, you ask 'Can it be that he who was born before all ages might be born a second time, and he be God?' But if all this is impossible, how do you think the creeds of the Churches were made? How could you recite them yourself? Let us compare what you said then with what you say now. You said before, *I believe in God, the Father, and in Jesus Christ, his Son, true God from true God, consubstantial with the Father; he came for our sake and was born of the Virgin Mary, he was crucified under Pontius Pilate and was buried.* But what do you say now? 'Imagine if we were to say, "I believe in God the Word, the Son of God, the only-begotten one born of the Father, consubstantial with the Father, who descended and was buried"—would not the very hearing of it wound our ears?' The harshness of your impious words might make us heated and immoderate in our reply, but we will restrain the bounds of our grief a little.

X. I will ask your own opinion: tell me, if a Jew or a pagan were to contradict the creed of the Catholic faith, do you think we ought to listen to him? Surely not! And what if a heretic or an apostate were to so the same? Much less would we listen to him, for it is far worse to abandon the truth you have once known than to deny it without ever having known it. But in you we see two characters, both catholic and apostate: you were a Catholic before, now an apostate! You decide which we should pursue, for you cannot bring forward one character in yourself without repudiating the other. Do you want to condemn your former self, to deny your Catholic creed, to deny what all confess and all believe? Why indeed? What a scandal, what an unbearable grief! What are you doing in the Catholic Church, you who lead Catholics astray? Why infest the assembly of the people when you deny that people's faith? How can you stand before the altar, how can you ascend the pulpit, how can you impose your impudent and outrageous words on the people of God? How can you sit on the throne, take on yourself the high priesthood, claim any authority? Why teach Christians when you yourself do not believe in Christ? You deny God himself, although you are in his temple—and after all that, O madness, you think you are a teacher and a bishop! It is God himself that you are rejecting, God himself, in your blindness, and you call yourself his priest!

But I am getting carried away by grief. What does the Creed say, the Creed that you recited yourself? *The Lord Jesus Christ true God from true God, consubstantial with the Father, through him the ages were created and all things made; he himself came for our sake and was born of the Virgin Mary.* If you said that God was born from Mary, how can you deny that Mary is the Mother of God? When you have said that God came, how can you deny that the one who came is God? You have recited the Creed, *I believe in Jesus Christ the Son of God, I believe in true God from true God, consubstantial with the Father, who came for our sake and was born of the Virgin Mary, crucified under Pontius Pilate and was buried.* But now you are saying, 'If we were to say, "I believe in God the Word, the Son of God, the only-begotten one born of the Father, consubstantial with the Father, who descended and was buried"—would not the very hearing of it wound our ears?' Don't you see that you are totally undermining every belief of the Catholic creed, of the Catholic sacraments? 'What a crime, what a wonder!' as Cicero said, 'let it be taken away to the end of the world!' (M. Tullius Cicero, *Actio in C. Verrem*, II, lib. I, 15). That would be appropriate for you, if you could be taken away to a desert where you would find no one to pervert! You think that our saving faith, our hope in the sacraments of the Church, is a 'saying that wounds your ears'. So how could you listen to it without damage to your ears when you came so eagerly to your baptism? Why were your ears not wounded when the teachers of the Church instructed you? You do not seem to have been injured when you used both ears and mouth, to speak what you heard others say, to hear yourself as you spoke. Where were those sensitive ears of yours then? Where those wounds you complain of? Why did you not then contradict them and object? No, it seems to be at your own convenience and whim that you can be a disciple of the Church when you choose, or her enemy; a Catholic when you choose, or an apostate. You are a powerful force indeed, for whichever way you choose to go the Church must follow; your whim is our rule of life, as you change your mind the human race must change, and become what you want, since you will not be what everyone else is. How astounding your authority is, if when you are no longer what you were, the world as well must cease to be what it was.

XI. But I suppose you will claim that you were a child when you were baptized, and unable to understand or object. True enough, your age at the time prevented you from protesting, though as a man you are able to contradict it, and die. And what would have happened if you had attempted to change anything or deny it while the bishop was teaching the creed to the people of God, and they were jubilant in response, in that church which was so faithful and devoted to Christ? Would they have listened to you? Would they not rather have driven you out at once for extermination, like some monstrous new breed of vermin! Not that God's people, pious and faithful as they are, would want to be contaminated with the blood of anyone, no matter how wicked, but the population of a great city, fired with the love of God, would be unable to restrain the heat of their faith if they saw anyone rising up against their God. But I concede your point: as an infant you were indeed unable to contradict the creed or refuse it: but why did you remain silent when you had grown up and were more robust? For you did grow up and become a man, and entered the ministry of the Church. Through all those years, and all the degrees of holy order, did you never come to understand the faith that you had taught for so long? You became Christ's deacon, and then his priest: if the rule of salvation was displeasing to you, why did you take on the dignity of the truth, whose profession you did not approve? You were, I suppose, a foreseeing man, simple in your religion, and determined to maintain the middle path, to retain both your blasphemous disbelief, and your Catholic status.

XII. A pain for you to hear, a wound to your ears, that God was born, that God suffered! Hear St Paul the Apostle describe your case: 'But we preach Christ crucified; unto the Jews indeed a stumbling-block, and unto the Gentiles foolishness; but unto them that are called, both Jews and Greeks, Christ, the power of God and the wisdom of God' (I Corinthians 1:23–4). What is this wisdom and power of God? God himself. And he proclaims Christ who was crucified as the power and the wisdom of God. Surely, then, if Christ is the wisdom of God, Christ is certainly God. 'We preach Christ crucified; unto the Jews indeed a stumbling-block, and unto the Gentiles foolishness.' It is the Cross of the Lord which the Gentiles think foolish, which scandalizes the Jews, and it has both effects on you. There is no foolishness greater than unbelief, no greater scandal than refusing to hear. Their ears were wounded by the proclamation of the suffering of God, as your ears are now. They thought it a pain to hear, just as you do now. As a result when they heard the name of Jesus Christ, as God and Lord, when the apostle preached Christ as God, they blocked the ears on their heads, just as you close the ears of your soul. Can we consider you both equal in your impiety? Hardly: we can blame you even more than they, for they denied him after his suffering had showed that he was really a man, while you deny him after his resurrection had demonstrated that he is God. Moreover they only persecuted him on earth, while you are persecuting him in heaven. Nay more, you are the worse and more cruel, for they denied him in ignorance, but you denied him after having had faith. They did not know the Lord, but you have confessed him to be God; they were under the restrictions of the Law, but you had made profession as a bishop. They denied one they considered to be a stranger to them, but you, him whose high priest you were. How unworthy, how unparalleled! You set yourself against him and persecute him, though you have enjoyed the dignity of his service!

XIII. You are using an argument which is most cynical and unworthy, in your denial and persecution of our Lord and God, when you claim that 'one who is born must be consubstantial with the parent.' I assert that this does not properly apply to the nativity of God, for in this case the birth was the initiative of the one being born, not of the one who gave birth. He was born as he willed to be, for it was his own choice to be born. But anyway, as you say, the one born should be consubstantial with the parent: I tell you that Our Lord Jesus Christ was consubstantial with the Father, and just as much so with his mother. He reflected in his own likeness the different natures of each of his parents: according to his divinity he was consubstantial with the Father, according to the flesh he was consubstantial with his mother. Nor was the one consubstantial with the Father a person different from he who was consubstantial with the mother, but it is the same Lord Jesus

Christ who is both born as man and is God, having in himself the natures of both parents. What was human in him reflected the likeness of his human mother; what was divine in him had the truth of God the Father.

XIV. Otherwise you would be creating two Christs, if it was not the same Christ who was born of Mary and was born of God. That is what the wicked Pelagians taught, asserting that it was a mere man who was born of the Virgin, calling him the instructor of the human race rather than our redeemer, for he did not grant men redemption of life, but only gave them an pattern of how to live. Thus men might follow him by doing as he did, and so arrive at the same state. Your heresy has the same origin, therefore, your error stems from the same root. They assert that a mere man was born of Mary, just as you do. They separate the Son of Man from the Son of God, and you do the same. They say that Christ became the Saviour at his baptism, you say that it was in his baptism that he was made the temple of God. They do not deny that he was made God after his passion, but you deny it even after his ascension. That then is the only difference between your perversity and theirs, that they appear to blaspheme the Lord on earth, while you blaspheme him also in heaven. We do not deny that you have surpassed and exceeded those you imitate. They do cease to deny his divinity at some stage, but you never. Nevertheless they should not be considered as having made an adequate profession of faith in conceding the honour of divinity to our Saviour after his passion, and admitting that he finally became God though they denied that he was before, since as it seems to me, anyone who denies God in part denies him totally; if you deny that he was always God, you are denying that he ever is. The same applies to you: even if you accept that our Lord Jesus Christ who was born of the Virgin Mary, is now truly God in heaven, yet unless you admit that he was always God, you are not admitting the truth. I suppose you want to be consistent, without changing or adapting your opinion: having said that it was a mere man who was born, you maintain that he is still not God. What an unheard-of and remarkable idea:

you join the heretics in saying he was a mere man, but you will not join them in confessing that he is now God!

XV. I had begun to say that you have made yourself two Christs, so I must explain what I mean by that. Tell me, then; since you separate Christ from the Son of God, how could you confess in the Creed that Christ was born of God? For you said, *I believe in God the Father, and in Christ Jesus, the Son of God.* So here you have Jesus Christ as the Son of God. But you say that the one born of Mary was not the same Son of God—so Christ, born of God, is not the same as the one born of Mary. Which means you consider there are two Christs. You do not deny the Christ in the Creed, and you assert that the Christ who was born of Mary, is other than the one you confess in the Creed. Are you saying perhaps that Christ was not born of God? But did you not say, in the Creed, *I believe in Jesus Christ, the Son of God*? You must either deny the Creed, or confess that the Son of God is Christ. And if you do confess, in the Creed, that Christ is the Son of God, it must follow that you admit that the same Christ, Son of God, was born of Mary. Otherwise you would be committing the blasphemy of saying that there are two Christs, if the one born of Mary is another one.

XVI. If your perverse lack of belief is not refuted by the faith of the Creed, will you not be overwhelmed by the light of truth and reason? Tell me, O heretic whoever you are! Surely we believe in the Trinity and acknowledge the Father, the Son and the Holy Ghost? There can be no doubt over the majesty of the Father and the Spirit, but you are denying the Son in saying that it is not the same one born of Mary who was begotten by God the Father. So tell me: if you do not deny that the only-begotten Son of God was born of God, who do you think the one born of Mary was? You tell me he was a mere man, and quote his own words, 'That which is born of the flesh is flesh' (John 3:6). But he cannot be called a mere man, for he was not begotten by the means of human generation alone: the angel said, 'that which is conceived in her is of the Holy Ghost' (Matthew 1:20). Even you, who deny all the mysteries of salvation, will not dare to deny that. And if he is born of the Holy Ghost, he cannot be called a mere man, for he was conceived by the inbreathing of God. He it is of whom St Paul said, he 'emptied himself, taking the form of a servant' (Philippians 2:7), and 'the Word was made flesh' (John 1:14). He 'humbled himself, becoming obedient unto death' (Philippians 2:8), and 'being rich, he became poor for our sakes' (II Corinthians 8:9). So tell me, who is this who was both born of the Holy Spirit, and conceived by the overshadowing of God? You will say, I suppose, that it was someone else. There are two persons: one who was begotten of God the Father in heaven, and another who was conceived by Mary at the inbreathing of God. Thus it comes about that you are introducing a fourth person, for although the words you use are that he was a mere man, in reality you mean that he was more than that, for you admit that he is to be honoured, venerated and adored, though not in the way you should. Therefore, if we should adore the Son of God who was born of the Father, and also adore the one who was born of Mary by the Holy Spirit, you have given us two persons to be honoured and venerated, dividing them to the extent that each is honoured in his own special way. Now you must understand that by doing this, by denying and dividing the Son of God from himself, you are doing your best to overthrow the entire mystery of the Godhead. By trying to insert a fourth person into the Trinity, you must see that you are effectively denying the Trinity altogether.

XVII. Besides this, when you deny that there is one Jesus Christ, the Son of God, you are denying everything. That is the nature of the theology of the Church and the Catholic Faith: if you deny part of the mystery of God you are unable to confess any other part. All points are so interconnected and interdependent that one cannot stand without the other, so that he who denies one point among them all can reap no advantage by believing in all the others. If you deny that Our Lord Jesus Christ is God, you have to deny the Son of God, and therefore even the Father. As the Word of God himself said, 'Whosoever denieth the Son, the same hath not the Father. He that confesseth the Son hath the Father also' (I John 2:23). When you deny the one who was begotten, you deny the one who begat him. When you deny the Son of God born in the flesh, it follows that you must deny him born in the Spirit, for it is the same person born in the flesh who was born first in the Spirit. And if you do not believe that he came forth in the flesh, you cannot believe that he suffered. If you do not believe in his passion, what follows? That you must disbelieve in the Resurrection, for our faith in the one who rose derives from our faith in the one who died. There can be no case for the resurrection unless you already believe that he died, so that if you deny that he suffered and died, you must deny that he rose from the depths. It follows that you must deny that he ascended, for there could be no ascension without the resurrection; if you do not believe that he rose, you cannot believe he ascended, for the Apostle says, 'He that descended is the same also that ascended' (Ephesians 4:10). Therefore, as far as you are concerned, the Lord Jesus Christ did not rise from the dead, nor did he ascend into heaven, nor does he sit at the right hand of God the Father, nor will he come to the day of the Last Judgment, as we hope for, nor will he judge the living and the dead.

XVIII. In your miserable and unlucky perversity, can you understand that you have totally nullified the entire faith of the Creed, and all effective hope in the sacraments? Yet you still presume to stand up in the Church and consider yourself a bishop, when you have denied all that your high priesthood was first based on! Return to the right path, accept again what you first believed, become wise again at last, as once you were. Return to yourself, if you ever had in yourself something to which you can return. Acknowledge the sacraments of your own salvation, through which you were made new and reborn. You have no less need of them now than then, for in penance they will restore you to the state you were given at the font. Hold to the full doctrine of the Creed: hold to the fullness of the truth of that faith. Believe in God the Father; believe in God the Son; in one who begat and in one begotten, [the same person, only-begotten and first-begotten]; Jesus Christ, the Lord of All, consubstantial with the Father; born in divinity, born in the body, of a twofold birth but one majesty. He who was born of the Father, the creator of all creatures, is the same as he who was afterwards born of the Virgin.

XIX. The fact that he was born of the flesh, and came in the flesh, was a beginning, not a diminution; he was but born, not changed. He remained in the form of God, but assumed too the form of a slave, and the weakness of his human demeanour did not detract from his nature as God. The power of his divinity remained entire and whole, while he did everything in his human body: this was to the advancement of man, not the diminution of God's majesty. When God came forth in human flesh, he was not born in the flesh in order that God should abide in him, but so that as God abode in himself, man might be God. For this reason, when Martha saw him with her physical eyes as a man, she discerned God with the eyes of her spirit, and said, 'Yea, Lord, I have believed that thou art Christ, the Son of the living God, who art come into this world' (John 11:27). Likewise Peter was inspired by the Holy Spirit so that when he looked externally at the Son of Man, he proclaimed the Son of God, in the words, 'Thou art Christ, the Son of the Living God' (Matthew 16:16). Thomas, too, when he touched the flesh believed that he was touching God, saying, 'My Lord and my God' (John 20:28).

All of these proclaimed, therefore, that there is one Christ, lest they make him two. Believe in him: believe that Jesus Christ is Lord of all, only-begotten, and first-begotten, the creator of all things, and also the preserver of mankind, the same who first founded the whole world and afterwards redeemed the human race. He remains with the Father and in the Father, consubstantial with the Father, as St Paul says, 'taking the form of a servant, he humbled himself unto death, even to the death of the cross' (Philippians 2:7–8). As the Creed says, *he was born of the Virgin Mary, he was crucified under Pontius Pilate and was buried; on the third day he rose according to the Scriptures, and ascended to heaven; he will*

come again to judge the living and the dead. This is our faith, this
is our salvation: we believe in our God and Lord Jesus Christ, the
same, before all things and after all things. As it is written, 'Jesus
Christ, yesterday and today; and the same for ever' (Hebrews 13:8).
By 'yesterday' he means all time past, in which he was born of the
Father before all beginnings. By 'today' he means the expanse of
this present age, in which he was a second time born, of the Virgin;
he suffered, and rose again. By 'the same for ever' he means to
indicate the whole vast expanse of eternity to come.

XX. So maybe you think that if I say that the one born at the end
of time from the Virgin is the same as he who was born of God the
Father before all things, I must conclude that God was enfleshed
before the beginning of the world. Yes, I say that he who was
always God became man later, and remains man ever after, since
he has been born. But I do not want you to be so confused in your
blind ignorance and error that you might think I am asserting
the man who was born of Mary existed before the creation of all
things, and that God had a body always, before the beginning of
the world. That is not what I am saying. I do not mean that the
man existed in God before he was born, but that after he was
born, God existed as man. The flesh which was derived from the
flesh of the Virgin did not always exist, but God, who did always
exist, came in human flesh of the flesh of the Virgin. The Word
was made flesh: he did not bring the flesh with him, but united
himself to human flesh through the power of his godhead. Tell
me: when and where was the Word made flesh? When did he
empty himself, taking the form of a slave? When was he made
poor, though he was rich? Surely it was in the sacred womb of the
Virgin, where he took flesh and as we are told the Word of God
was made flesh. When he came forth he truly took on the form of
a servant; when he was fastened to the Cross in his human nature
he became poor, reduced to poverty by his bodily suffering, though
he was rich in his divine majesty. Your opinion is different: that
it was afterwards that divinity came upon him, as if to any of the
prophets or saints, in that the Word is made flesh in any of those

in whom he deigns to dwell; he empties himself taking the form of a slave in any of them. Which would mean that there was nothing new or exceptional about Christ: nothing unique or marvellous about his conception, his nativity or his death.

XXI. To return to what I was saying before: since the truth is as I have stated it, how comes it that the Scriptures tell us that Jesus Christ, whom you assert to be a mere man, even before he was born of the Virgin, existed always; how was he proclaimed as God before the ages by the prophets and apostles? Paul says, 'one Lord Jesus Christ, by whom are all things' (I Corinthians 8:6), and elsewhere, 'in him were all things created in heaven and on earth, visible and invisible' (Colossians 1:16). The Creed, also, which is woven together from human and divine authority, says, *I believe in God the Father, and in the Lord Jesus Christ, his only-begotten Son, the first-born of all creation; ... true God from true God ... through him the ages were assembled, and all things made; he came for our sake and was born of the Virgin Mary, he was crucified and was buried ...*

XXII. Now our belief is that the humanity of the Lord did not exist at all before the Virgin conceived and gave birth, whereas you have to explain how Christ, whom you call a mere man, could be described in Holy Scripture as God without beginning. When we read about such a close union of man and God, does it mean that the man existed always, co-eternal with God, and God could afterwards be seen suffering along with man? For we cannot believe that man can be without beginning, or that God can suffer. The truth is, as we have already established in what is written above, that God, united to man, that is to his own body, permits no distinction to be made in human thought between the man and God. Nor did God will it to be possible for anyone to think that one person is the Son of Man, another the Son of God. Throughout Holy Scripture the humanity of the Lord is connected and incorporated into the divinity, so that no one can distinguish the manhood from the divinity in time, nor separate

God from his humanity during the Passion. If you consider the expanse of time, you will always find the Son of Man with the Son of God: if you consider the passion, you will find the Son of God ever with the Son of Man. Christ, both Son of Man and Son of God, is so united in himself that as far as the words of Scripture are concerned you cannot ever separate the humanity from the divinity in time, nor the divinity from the humanity in the Passion. Thus it is true that 'No man hath ascended into heaven, but he that descended from heaven, the Son of Man who is in heaven' (John 3:13). On this occasion the Son of God was speaking on earth, and gave witness that the Son of Man was in heaven: the same Son of Man that he said would ascend into heaven, he tells us had already descended from heaven. In another place, 'If then you shall see the Son of Man ascend up where he was before' (John 6:63). He names the one who was born of man, and tells us that he had always existed in the realm above. St Paul, also, when he considers the expanse of time, proclaims that all things were made through Christ, saying, 'One Lord Jesus Christ, by whom are all things' (I Corinthians 8:6). When he considers the Passion, he says that it was the Lord of glory who was crucified; 'for if they had known it,' he says, 'they would never have crucified the Lord of glory' (I Corinthians 2:8). It is the same in the Creed, which gives testimony to *Our Lord Jesus Christ, his only-begotten Son, the first-born, … true God from true God, consubstantial with the Father, the creator of all things, … born of the Virgin Mary, he was crucified and was buried …* The Son of God and Son of Man are thus so closely united, manhood and divinity made one, so that neither in time nor during the Passion can there be any division. Our Lord Jesus Christ is shown to be God through the expanse of time, and to be man through the endurance of the Passion; while we cannot talk of a humanity without beginning or a godhead suffering, yet we proclaim a man who ever pre-existed, and a God who died, in the one Lord Jesus Christ. See now how Christ is all things; his name indicates both natures, for he was born both as man and as God. He contains all things in himself so that nothing can be found missing from his name. It is not that

before the Virgin gave birth the manhood had the same eternity as
the godhead, but that in the womb of the Virgin God was united
with man: thus it came to pass that in Christ one nature cannot
possibly be named without the other.

XXIII. It follows that whatever you say about Our Lord Jesus
Christ you say about him in his wholeness: you name the Son of
Man in the Son of God, and the Son of God in the Son of Man.
This is a sort of *synecdoche*, the figure of speech by which you
understand the whole from a part, and a part takes its name
from the whole. The Lord frequently uses this figure of speech in
Holy Scripture, to teach us that, as it can be used in other cases,
so he would have us use it in his own. In no other way do the
sacred writings designate days, things, men or times. For instance,
when God foretold that Israel would serve the Egyptians for four
hundred years, he said to Abraham, 'Know thou beforehand that
thy seed shall be a stranger in a land not their own, and they shall
bring them under bondage, and afflict them four hundred years'
(Genesis 15:13). If you consider the whole time about which God
was speaking, it was more than four hundred, but if you mean
the actual time during which they were in bondage, it was less.
Unless you understand that God stated the period of time in the
form of *synecdoche*, you might think the word of God was untrue,
which is repugnant to Christians. From the time that the divine
words were spoken, the whole span of time was more than four
hundred years; the time of bondage much less: thus the part stood
for the whole, and the whole was understood from the part. A
similar case is that of the interlude of days and nights: 'one day'
can be understood to mean both a day and a night, so that the
whole length of time is indicated by one part of it. In this way can
be explained the apparently obscure passage about the duration
of the Lord's Passion. The Lord used the example of the prophet
Jonah to foretell that the Son of Man would be 'in the heart of
the earth three days and three nights' (Matthew 12:40), yet after
the sixth day of the week on which he was crucified, there ensued
only a single day and two nights during which he was among the

dead—so how can the word of God be found true? Assuredly by this figure of *synecdoche*, so that we attribute the previous night to the day on which he was crucified, and the following day to the night on which he rose; thus if you add the night which came before the first day, and the day which followed the third night, nothing is missing from the extent of time designated by its parts.

Holy Scripture is full of examples like this, but it would take too long to go over them all. As the Psalm says, 'What is man that thou art mindful of him?' (Psalm 8:5) The whole is understood from the part when one man is named and an entire race of people indicated. Thus when Achab sinned, the whole people are said to have sinned; the whole nation are accused, and the individual specified from the whole. John the Precursor of the Lord said, 'After me there cometh a man, who was made before me; because he was before me' (John 1:30). How can he say that he was coming after him, when he states that he existed before him? If this is to be understood of the man, who was born after him, how could he have existed before him? If of the Word, how could he be coming after him? Only because the man that came after, and the Word that existed before, are manifest in the one Lord Jesus Christ. Thus it happens that one and the same Lord existed before him, and came after him; according to the flesh he was younger than John, according to his divinity he is older than us all. John named only the man, and indicated both the man and the Word. Our Lord Jesus Christ, the Son of God, comprised both man and Word, so by naming one of these he indicated the whole.

What more need I say? I think the day is too short to attempt to collect up and expound everything I could say on this matter. What I have said will be enough, at least for this part of the argument, both to expound the Creed, and to put forth my case, and to fill up the volume.

❖

✟ Book Seven ✟

I. Now there happens to me what happens to those who have finished a sea crossing: they fear the shoals that lie in front of the harbour, or the rocks on the adjoining shores. I have kept until last the calumnies of the heretics, and now that I have arrived at the end of the task I set myself, I am beginning to fear that end which I had been so longing to reach. But the Psalmist says, 'The Lord is my helper: I will not fear what man can do unto me' (Psalm 117:6). We need not fear the snares which the heretics have laid maliciously before us, nor the paths beset with fierce thorns on every side, for though they make the way rough, they cannot block it. While they do provide us with the labour of clearing them, they fail to make us fear that we cannot pass. These things form obstacles, and we make our way with difficulty along the right path, but they can only delay us, they cannot block the way. It is our task and duty to clear them out of the way, but we need not fear any real difficulty.

So let us raise our hand against the monstrous head of that deadly serpent, and deal with all the constricting force of the vast coils of that tortuous body; again and again let us pray to you, Lord Jesus, whom we ever invoke, 'that speech may be given me, that I may open my mouth with confidence' (Ephesians 6:19), 'unto the pulling down of fortifications, destroying counsels, and every being that exalteth itself against the knowledge of God; and bringing into captivity every understanding unto thine own obedience' (II

Corinthians 10:4–5). Truly he who begins by being your captive is free indeed. Be with us as we embark on your own work, stand by your own as they struggle beyond their own strength. Grant that we may defeat the new dragon that gapes upon us, that we may break the necks that swell with deadly venom, for it is you who make it possible for the feet of the faithful to walk unharmed over serpents and scorpions, to 'walk upon the asp and the basilisk, to trample under foot the lion and the dragon' (Psalm 90:13). Grant us the fearless confidence of innocence, that 'the sucking child shall play on the hole of the asp: and the weaned child shall trust his hand into the den of the basilisk' (Isaiah 11:8). Grant that we too may thrust our innocent hands into the dens of this monstrous and wicked basilisk. If the asp has already made itself a hole, and found a lurking place or den in human minds, and laid there her eggs or left the slimy trail of her passing, take away from us all the vile contagion of that loathly worm. Drag out the uncleanness of unbelief which has been brought in; cleanse our minds, if they reek of evil, with the fans of your sacred purification; turn the dens of robbers into houses of prayer. Those places which are now, as Scripture says, the lairs of urchins and onocentaurs, of the hairy ones and other varied monsters, make resplendent with the gifts of your Holy Spirit, that is the beauty of faith and devotion. Just as you turned the temples of demons into shrines of virtue by ejecting the worship of idols and destroying their images, as you sent the shining rays of your light into the dens of serpents and scorpions, and changed the cells of error and vice into chambers of splendour and beauty; in the same way pour the lights of your mercy and truth into all those whose eyes have been obscured by dark and heretical falsehood. Thus they may look on the great and saving mystery of your Incarnation with pure and unsullied light, and recognize you, brought forth from the sacred womb of the immaculate Virgin as true man, and also as true God who existed ever before.

II. Before I begin to deal with matters which I have not touched on in the previous books, I feel I should turn to something I have already promised to answer, so that once I have concluded my obligations, I may be free to move on to new points, having dealt with the ones I had undertaken to do. Our new serpent, hissing against the Church of God, tried to destroy our faith in the nativity by saying, 'No one brings forth one older than herself'. To begin with, I think you are ignorant not only of what you are saying but what your source was, for if you knew what you were saying, and from what source, you would never have impugned the birth of the Only-begotten God with such a trivial human thought. Nor would you have assailed with human limitations one who was born without human conception, or limited God's omnipotence with earthly difficulties, had you only realized that nothing is impossible to God. 'No one brings forth one older than herself', you say. Tell me what cases you are talking about, what sort of beings are you trying to define? Are you attempting to legislate for men or beasts, birds or cattle? Of these, and creatures like them, you could say what you have said, for none of these is able to bring forth one older than itself, for those which have already been born cannot return into the position of being brought forth in a second creation. Therefore none of them brings forth an older specimen, since they cannot beget anything older, bringing to birth being dependent on the possibility of conception. But do you think that something which applies to the reproduction of terrestrial animals can apply to the nativity of Almighty God? Can you restrict him, who is himself the author of nature, under the limitations of human nature? Don't you see, as I have said before, that you are ignorant of what you are saying and whence, if you compare creatures with the Creator, and assess the omnipotence of God by the example of things which would not themselves exist at all did not their being derive from God? God came to us as he willed, when he willed, and from her whom he willed. He was not restricted by time, person or human custom, or by the example of other things; the law of creatures could not obstruct him, for he is the creator of them all. He had the ability to do at once what he willed, for the power existed in his will. Do you want to know how great the omnipotence of God is? I believe that God can do with his creatures what you do not believe he can do with himself. Any animal, which brings forth offspring younger than itself, could generate offspring much older than itself if God willed it. Food and drink could be turned into new creatures, if God so willed. Even water, which has flowed from the beginning of time, and which is used by every living thing, could take solid form, if God willed, within a womb and be brought to birth. Who can set a limit to the sacred work, or constrain God's providence? Who can say to him, as the Scripture says, 'What art thou making?' (Isaiah 45:9) If you do not agree that God can do all things, then you may deny that when God was born something older than herself could be born of Mary; but if nothing is impossible to God, why object that there is an impossibility in his own coming, if you agree that nothing at all is impossible for him?

III. Your second perverse saying, (whether a blasphemous calumny or a calumnious blasphemy), is 'what is born must be consubstantial with the parent'. It is similar to the previous point, different more in words than in substance. In dealing with the nativity of God, you are saying that Mary could not bring to birth one more powerful than she, which is much the same as saying she could not bring forth one older than she, as you said before. Hence take the same answer as to the previous objection, or apply what I should say now to the other as well. You have said, 'what is born must be consubstantial with the parent'. If you are thinking of earthly creatures, that is true enough; but if you are thinking of the birth of God, why apply examples from nature to his nativity? What has been decreed cannot stand in the way of the one who decrees, but why should not the one who decrees control what he has himself decreed? Do you want further proof that your calumnies are not only disrespectful but also irrelevant, the ramblings of someone who has no clear vision of God's omnipotence? If you think like things can only come from like, tell me where that inexplicable multitude of quails came from, which were suddenly brought forth in the desert to feed the Israelites. We do not read that they had previously been born from parents, in some other place, but that they arrived suddenly. And that heavenly food, where did that come from, dropping onto the Hebrew encampment for forty years? Did manna generate manna?

But these are Old Testament miracles: how about the New? More than once Our Lord Jesus Christ fed a vast crowd of followers in the wilderness with a few loaves and some small fishes. The explanation for the abundance was not in the food itself, but it was some invisible secret cause that fed the hungry, especially since what was left over was much more than what had been supplied for the feeding. By what means did this come to pass, that when those who ate had had enough, the food was ample for a marvellous amount to remain over? We read that in Galilee wine was once brought forth from water. Tell me how one nature could bring forth something of a different nature, especially since, as in the case of Our Lord's nativity, a much more noble substance derived from a less valuable one. How did the noble flavour and taste of wine derive from simple water? How could one thing be drawn out, a different one poured in? Did the cistern, or the well, have the property that water drawn out of it would become fine wine? Was it a characteristic of the jars, some skill of the servants? None of these! How can the explanation of what happened not be accepted by the heart when the truth of the matter is recognized in the strength of the conscience?

In the Gospel we read that mud was placed on the eyes of the blind man, and when it was washed off, his eyes were reborn. Did the water have the quality of bringing forth sight? Did mud naturally being forth light? Not at all: for water can do nothing for blindness, and mud is a positive obstacle to sight. How could something which had the ability to harm be able to serve for healing? How could what would be an obstacle to the healthy be able to serve for a remedy? You will tell me that this was the result of the power of God, the healing came from God. In all the cases I have cited it was God's omnipotence that operated, for he is powerful to make new things out of unlikely material, to turn dangerous things into means of healing. Things which were naturally incapable or useless he can turn to efficacious uses.

IV. We must confess that the same applies to the birth of Our Lord as to all matters else: believe that God was born, as he willed to be; for you cannot deny that he could do whatever he willed, unless you imagine that the power which he had in regards to all else failed him in his own case. Could omnipotence which reached to the ends of the universe fail him in his own nativity? Your objection to the Lord's nativity was 'No one brings forth one older than herself'; and to the coming to birth of the omnipotent God, 'What is born must be consubstantial with the parent'. You are accustomed to treat men according to the laws of human nature: can you restrict God within earthly limitations and object that anything is impossible for him? You apply a common condition to all who are to be born, the same laws to all who are brought to birth, as if it were impossible for anything to apply to a single man among the entire human race if God had forbidden it to apply to all. You do not understand whom you are talking about, you do not see of whom you are speaking. He is the author of all restrictions, of all the laws of nature; he it is who decides what any man can do and what he cannot do. He has established the limits in both cases, that of being able to achieve something, and of being unable to go further. What madness it is to make the objection that something is impossible for him, when all possibility derives from him! If you judge the person of the Lord by the standards of earthly weakness, and measure the omnipotence of God by human reason, you would find that no aspect of bodily suffering can be appropriate to God. If it seems likely that Mary was unable to give birth to God who is older than she, how could it be likely that God might be crucified by men? But God himself foretold that he would be crucified: 'Shall a man afflict God? For you afflict me' (Malachi 3:8). If the Lord is not believed to have been born of the Virgin, because he who was born was older than the one who gave birth, how can we believe that God has blood? Yet the elders of Ephesus were told: 'Rule the church of God which he hath purchased with his own blood' (Acts 20:28). How can the author of life be considered to have lost his life? For St Peter said, 'the author of life you killed' (Acts

3:15). No one living on the earth can also be in heaven, but the Lord himself said, 'the Son of Man who is in heaven' (John 3:13). If, then, you do not think God was born of the Virgin, for the one born must be consubstantial with the one giving birth, how can you believe that anything of one nature came forth from anything of a different nature? Therefore, according to you, the sudden wind did not produce the quails, the manna did not descend, the wine was not produced from water, the many thousands of men were not fed on the scanty food, light did not appear to the blind man after the mud was applied. All these things would seem to be incredible and contrary to reason, did we not believe that God had done them, so how can you deny that he could do something in his own nativity which you admit he did in these other miracles? Was he really unable to make special provision for his own coming and birth, such that he did not refuse to make for the healing and benefit of men?

V. It would be tedious and verbose to say more about this matter. Nevertheless, to refute your inept and insane saying, 'What is born must be consubstantial with the parent', in other words that nothing can bring forth something unlike itself, I will give you a few examples of earthly creatures to show that many things are born from something unlike themselves. Not that there can or should be any real comparison, but that you should be in no doubt that what you see happening in transitory earthly matters can be the truth in the case of that sacred nativity.

Take bees, small creatures indeed, but wise and prudent: we read that they derive from a most unlikely origin and nature. Despite being creatures of marvellous ingenuity, endowed with foresight as well as sense, they are generated out of flowers selected from certain plants. Can you think of a better example to mention and discuss? Animals are born out of dust; things with understanding out of things senseless. Who is the workman, who the designer? Who formed their bodies and animated their minds? Who gave them the buzzing noise with which they communicate with each other? Who arranged and formed their elegant limbs, their versatile mouths, their delicate wings? They have many things in common with mankind: skill, anger, foresight, movement, repose, agreement, dissent, warfare, peace, government, deployment, rank, authority and all: who taught them these? Whose example, model and instruction made them behave thus? Did they receive them from their fathers' seed? Or in their mothers' wombs, from their mothers' bodies? They knew no womb, derived from no seed. It was only the produce of flowers that congealed in the cells, so that the bees emerged by some marvellous process. The womb of a mother contributed nothing to these little ones, for bees are not born from bees. They are workers, not mothers. They produce their young from the flowers of plants: and what is there in common between plants and animals? But I think you know who it was who devised these things: go, then, and consider, could the Lord apply to his own birth what you see him doing for these tiny creatures?

After that it would be superfluous to add any more examples, but even if not necessary to convince you, they will add to our evidence. We observe that the air may suddenly form locusts which fill the earth. Can you find their seed, their birth, their progenitors? You can see that they appear from the air which gives them birth. Can you say of all these creatures that 'What is born must be consubstantial with the parent'? You will appear as ridiculous in asserting that as you were found insane in denying the Lord's nativity. And what follows? Need we go on, do you think? Let us give another example: it is well known that basilisks, a type of serpent, are generated out of the eggs of the bird that the Egyptians call the *ibis*. What is there in common, what resemblance is there between a bird and a reptile? Why is what is born not consubstantial with the parent? Those who beget do not do so deliberately, those which are born know nothing of it, but it happens for unknown reasons according to an inexplicable and complicated law of natural generation. Can you really still bring out your trivial earthly objections against the Lord's nativity, while being unable to explain something as simple as the way in which basilisks are born? They are born at his will, his command, for everything happens at his bidding, and his power is over all: nothing can contradict him, nothing obstruct him, and his will is sufficient for everything to be possible to happen.

VI. It is time now to expose your remaining secret and insidious blasphemies, for much as we should like to, we cannot ignore them lest they deceive the ignorant. In one of your pestilential writings you assert as follows: 'Man being the image of the divine nature, and the devil having cast him down in the Fall, God grieved over his image, as the Emperor did over his statues, and has restored the fallen image: without seed he formed a being in the Virgin, just like Adam who was born without seed, and he raised up human nature through a human being, 'for as by a man came death, by a man came also the resurrection of the dead' (I Corinthians 15:21)'.

They tell me that the practice of poisoners is to mix honey in the vessels in which they confect their venom, so that the danger is concealed by sweetness, and the victim may be deceived by the taste of honey till he perishes by the poison. You do the same in your words, 'Man being the image of the divine nature, and the devil having cast him down in the Fall, God grieved over his image, as the Emperor did over his statues.' You have lined the rim of your poisoned cup with the sweetness of honey, so that men may drink the whole draught, tasting the allurement and failing to notice the danger. You put forward the name of God, to lie under cover of religion; you begin with holy things, to persuade us to evil; you confess God to the effect that you may deny the one you confess. Who fails to notice your aim, your intention? You say, indeed, 'God grieved over his image, as the Emperor did over his statues, and has restored the fallen image: without seed he formed a being in the Virgin, just like Adam who was born without seed, and he raised up human nature through a human being, 'for as by a man came death, by a man came also the resurrection of the dead'.' You say this, you sly deceiver, in such a carefully prepared manner, in such smooth words, that beginning with the name of God you may arrive at the mention of man; you abuse him with the reproach of being a mere man, after beginning by granting him the honour of God, by pretending to be humble. You tell us that the devil threw down the image of God in the Fall, and God's love restored it, 'he has restored the fallen image'. How subtle your words, 'he restored the fallen image', for you are trying to convince us that there was no more to him in whom the image was restored, than there was in the original image to which the restoration referred. In this way you want the Lord to be nothing other than Adam was, he who restored the image no more than he who caused it to fall. The words that follow reveal your aims and intentions, when you say, 'without seed he formed a being just like Adam who was born without seed, and he raised up human nature through a human being.' You tell us that Our Lord Jesus was exactly like Adam in every way: the one was born without seed, so was the other; the one was a mere man, the other merely a man. It is clear from this that you took great care not to let Our Lord Jesus Christ appear in any way greater or better than Adam, for you put them together under the same standard in such a way that it seems you think Adam would be dishonoured if anyone were to exceed him in any way.

VII. 'For as by a man came death, by a man came also the resurrection of the dead' (I Corinthians 15:21). Are you attempting to support your perverse wickedness by calling an apostle to witness? Are you defiling the Vessel of Election with the stain of your impiety? It appears that since you do not understand the author of your salvation, you have to make the Apostle appear to deny his God as well. But if you like using texts from St Paul, why have you cited only one and stopped there, why not add these others as well? 'Paul, an apostle, not of men, neither by man, but by Jesus Christ' (Galatians 1:1). 'We speak wisdom among the perfect ... which none of the princes of this world knew. For if they had known it, they would never have crucified the Lord of glory' (I Corinthians 2:6, 8). 'For in him dwelleth all the fullness of the Godhead corporeally' (Colossians 2:9). 'One Lord Jesus Christ, by whom are all things' (I Corinthians 8:6). Do you approve of the Apostle only in parts, and reject other parts? Do you accept him only when he calls Christ a man, because of the context, and repudiate him when he calls him God? St Paul does not deny that Jesus is a man, but he confesses that that same man is God. He proclaims that the resurrection of the human race came about through man, to confirm that it was God who rose in that man. Look and see: he proclaims that he who rose is God, he bears witness that he who was crucified is the Lord of glory.

VIII. Nevertheless you have granted some extra dignity to Our Lord Jesus, so as not to think of him just as one of the herd: you grant him the honour of a holy man, but refuse him the divinity of being true man and true God. What is it you are saying? 'God formed the Lord's incarnation, and we honour the *Theodochos*, the form of the God-receiver, as one form of divinity; he is like a statue inseparable from the divine will, the image of the hidden God.' You said earlier that Adam was the image of God: now you call Christ the image. If the one is a statue, so is the other. But we must thank you on behalf of the honour of God, for your grant of honour to the *Theodochos*, the form of the God-receiver along with God. But this is no honour, rather an insult! You are not granting the honour of divinity to Our Lord Jesus Christ, you are denying it. Your subtle but impious argument is that he should be honoured along with God, in order that you may not confess that he is God: the very point which seems, wrongly, to link them together actually separates them. When you say in your blasphemy that he should be honoured along with God, not worshipped as God, you are granting him close association with God but taking away the reality of divinity. How wicked you are, how sly, you enemy of God! You are trying to get away with denying him while pretending to honour him. 'Let us honour him,' you say, 'as the statue inseparable from the divine will, as the image of the hidden God.' What benefit will that confer on us, through his mercy, to honour the Creator and our Redeemer, the Lord Jesus Christ! But if we have been redeemed by him from eternal death, shall we call our Redeemer a statue? Is it a worthy response to his loving beneficence, is it worthy obedience and worship, to try to take away from him that majesty which he did not hesitate to lay aside for our sake?

IX. Perhaps you will try to excuse the insult you have offered the Lord in taking away his honour with the pretext that he is 'the image of the unseen God'. In calling him an image, you are certainly derogating from his dignity as unseen God, for David says, 'God shall come manifestly: our God shall come, and shall not keep silence' (Psalm 49/50:3). He came indeed, and was not silent, for as soon as he was born he proclaimed that coming through witnesses both human and divine; he was manifested by a star, adored by the magi, announced by angels. What more could you want? Now that his voice is silent on earth, his honour shouts from the heavens. Are you saying that he was hidden in himself, or is it you that are hiding God? Did not the prophets foretell him, the patriarchs, the whole law of the universe? Those who announced to everyone that he was coming did not say that he would be hiding. You must be blind in your error, if you are looking for a reason to blaspheme and failing to find one. You claim that he was hidden even after his coming: but I tell you that he was not hidden even before he came. Think of that great patriarch, who was given a new name after his vision of the presence of God, and rose to the title of Israel instead of being named the 'supplanter'—was it a secret from him that God would be born of a virgin? He acknowledged the mystery of the Incarnation to come, under the guise of the man that wrestled with him; he said, 'I have seen God face to face, and my soul has been saved' (Genesis 32:30). What was it he saw, that he might believe it was God he saw? Did God manifest himself in thunders and lightning? Did the face of divinity appear in splendour as the heavens burst open? None of these: what he saw was a man, but he recognized him as God. How worthy he was of the name he was given! With inner sight more than outer he deserved the dignity of the title granted him by God. He saw what looked like a man wrestling with him, and proclaimed that he saw God. He knew indeed that the human in appearance was God in truth, for the God who was then seen in appearance would later come in the true nature of that appearance. Need we be surprised that the mighty patriarch believed without doubt, for God showed himself to him so clearly that he could say, 'I have seen God face to face, and my soul has been saved.' How did God show him the presence of his divinity so clearly that he might say the face of God had been shown him? It was only a man that appeared to him, as it seemed, a man whom he had overcome in wrestling. But God did this to give in advance sufficient indication for no one to doubt that God was born of a man, for the patriarch had already seen God in human form.

X. But why am I taking so long over one example as if there were not many more? Could it ever have escaped men's notice that God would come in the flesh? The prophet indeed spoke openly about it, as if addressing the whole human race: 'Behold your God' (Isaiah 40:9); 'Lo, this is our God' (Isaiah 25:9); 'God the Mighty, the Father of the world to come, the Prince of Peace ... There shall be no end of ... his kingdom' (Isaiah 9:6–7). And once he had already come, did his coming ever escape those who publicly proclaimed that he had come? Was Peter ignorant of the coming of God, when he said, 'Thou art Christ, the Son of the Living God'? (Matthew 16:16). Was Martha unaware of what she was saying, what she believed, when she said, 'Yea, Lord, I have believed that thou art the Christ, the Son of the living God, who art come into this world'? (John 11:27). And all those who were begging him to cure diseases, to restore limbs, to raise the dead: were they asking this of human weakness, or of the omnipotence of God?

XI. When the devil was tempting Our Lord, with all his unlawful wiles, all his evil skills, what was it that he suspected, although unsure? What did he want to find out by tempting him? What was his motive other than to search out God in the form of lowly man? Had he not already discovered that from previous evidence? Was he not aware in which human body God had come? No indeed:

but he was compelled by the evidence of great signs, by the great things he had witnessed, by the very words of Truth himself, to suspect the reality he was investigating. He had once heard John the Baptist say, 'Behold the Lamb of God. Behold him who taketh away the sin of the world' (John 1:29). Again he heard him say, 'I ought to be baptized by thee, and comest thou to me?' (Matthew 3:14) And when the dove descended from heaven and hovered over the head of the Lord, it gave a clear and obvious proof that this was God. Then there was a voice sent by God which compelled him to know the truth, speaking neither in parables nor symbols, but in words, 'Thou art my beloved Son, in thee I am well pleased' (Mark 1:11). Therefore, although the devil saw the appearance of a man in Jesus, he tested the Son of God, saying, 'If thou be the Son of God, command that these stones be made bread' (Matthew 4:3). Did the sight of a man dispel the devil's suspicion that this was God, that he should imagine the man he was looking at could not be God? No indeed: that is why he said, 'If thou be the Son of God, command that these stones be made bread.' He was in no doubt that it was possible, which is why he was investigating whether it was so; his concern was over the reality, he was not sure that it was impossible.

XII. The devil knew indeed that Our Lord Jesus Christ had been born of Mary, that he had been wrapped in swaddling clothes and laid in a manger, that his childhood had been in poverty among men and his infancy lacking even the usual attendants at his cradle. He had no doubt that he possessed real flesh, was really born as a man. But why did this not make him confident? Why did he suspect that he whom he knew to be man could really have been God? Learn this, in your rabid madness, your insane impiety; learn this from the devil himself, how to lessen your infidelity! He said, 'If thou be the Son of God', but you are saying 'thou art not the Son of God'. You are denying what he was enquiring about. There has been no one before you found to exceed the impiety of the devil, for what he confessed was possible for the Lord, you do not believe to have been possible.

XIII. Perhaps his suspicions were then allayed; perhaps he ceased to wonder, having exhausted all temptations and failed to have any effect. But no, that suspicion remained with him always, even until the Lord's crucifixion, growing in him as his fears mounted. And even then he did not cease to suspect that he was the Son of God although he saw his persecutors being so strong against him. The subtle foe, observing signs of his divinity even during his bodily passion, was compelled to consider whether he was God, although he would much rather have thought him a man. However much he might have preferred to believe the opposite, he was forced by the clear evidence of events to accept what he dreaded. We should not be surprised: he may have seen him spat upon and scourged, laden with reproaches and fastened to the Cross, but among the indignities of these afflictions he could observe the abundance of divine power, for he saw the veil of the temple rent, the sun obscured, the day darkened, as all things reacted to the virtue of that Passion, all things that were ignorant of God came to acknowledge the operation of divinity. Seeing this, the devil was afraid, and attempted to make certain whether he was God, even in the midst of his human death, and spoke through those who had crucified him, 'If he be the Son of God, ... let him now come down from the Cross; and we will believe him' (Matthew 27:40, 42). He realized that our Lord and God was working the redemption and salvation of humanity through the suffering of his body, and that even as he himself was being destroyed and subjected, so we were being redeemed and saved. The enemy of the human race longed with all his being to obstruct what was happening, realizing that it was being done for our redemption. 'If he be the Son of God, let him come down from the cross, and we will believe him.' What he wanted was for the Lord to be provoked by this rebuke into abandoning the mystery for the sake of avenging his own suffering. So you see the Lord was called the Son of God even while he hung upon the Cross, you can see how they suspected the truth of what they said. Learn then, as I said before, either from the persecutors or from the devil himself, to believe in the Son of God. Has anyone ever equalled the infidelity of the devil? Has anyone surpassed it? But he suspected that Christ was the Son of God, even while he was suffering death: you deny it even after the resurrection! He detected that Christ was God, although he had concealed himself; but even though he has revealed himself, you deny him.

XIV. You attack God with Holy Scripture, and try to bring his own witnesses against him. What is the result? You are an opponent not only of God but also of his evidences. One should not be surprised: if you are unable to do what you intend, you have to do what you can; if you cannot turn the sacred text against God, you distort it as much as you can. You tells us that Paul was lying when he said of Christ that he was, 'without mother, without genealogy ...' (Hebrews 7:3). Now I ask you, whom would you like Paul to be speaking about? About the Son and Word of God, or about Christ whom you distinguish from the Son of God and consider a mere man in your blasphemy? If it is about Christ, whom you call a mere man, how could a man be born without a mother, and without a mother's genealogy? But if it is about the Word of God, the Son of God, how do you explain that the same Apostle whom you dare to call as your own witness, in the same passage and the same verse that you have cited as saying he was without a mother, tells us also that he was without a father. The text is, 'Without father, without mother, without genealogy ...' If you use the Apostle as your witness, you are saying absurdly that the Son of God, whom you say has no mother, has no father either. Look: your efforts in perverse blasphemy, on which you rely so wickedly, lead you to say what no one has ever said before, unless they were raving, that the Son of God has no mother, and you would deny him a father as well. I am not sure whether this is wickedness or stupidity: for it is both stupid and wicked to give the name of Son and to take away the name of Father. You claim you are neither denying nor taking away—then what madness has brought you to cite that text and say that he did not have a mother, which makes you appear to say that he has no father either? It is the same text that says he is without father as well as without mother; it must follow that if you understand it to mean he is without mother, you have to believe he was without a father as well. You did not realize that when you were so quick to deny God; by quoting an incomplete text, though there is more of it, you did not see that anyone could open the sacred volume and easily refute your audacious deceit. How foolish, how stupid you were in your blasphemy! Could you not see what was bound to happen? Did you not understand that anyone can read? In trying to cover up what you had come to realize, you thought you could cover up what was there for all to read; in losing the ability of your mind's eye, you thought everyone had lost the use of the eyes in their heads to read by. Listen, heretic, to what you tried to appropriate; listen to the complete text, which you quoted in a truncated form. The Apostle was trying to instruct everyone about the twofold nativity of God, showing that the Lord was born in divinity and in the flesh. He said, 'without father, without mother,' for one refers to the divine birth, the other to the human. As he was generated without a mother in his divinity, so he was without a father in his humanity. Thus he was neither without father nor mother, and at the same time was without both father and mother. He who was begotten of the Father, you see, had no mother; he was born of his mother, without a father. In each nativity he had one of the two, and was without the other. His birth in divinity needed no mother, in his physical birth he was sufficient unto himself without a father. Therefore the Apostle can say he was 'without mother, without genealogy.'

XV. But how can the apostle say that the Lord was 'without genealogy', when St Matthew's Gospel begins with the genealogy of the Saviour, 'The book of the generation of Jesus Christ, the son of David, the son of Abraham' (Matthew 1:1)? The evangelist says he had a genealogy, the Apostle that he had not; according to the Evangelist he had ancestry through his mother, according to the Apostle he had none through his father. The Apostle was right to say, 'without father, without mother, without genealogy' (Hebrews 7:3), for in that he considers him as without mother, there he notes that he is without genealogy. Because of the twofold nativity of the Lord, the writings of the evangelist and the apostle agree. According to the evangelist he had a genealogy, without a father, being born in the flesh; according to the Apostle he did not, for the Lord was begotten in his divinity without a mother. As the prophet Isaiah said, 'Who shall declare his generation?' (Isaiah 53:8).

XVI. Now, O heretic, why do you not quote the entire uncorrupted text that you read? You can see that the Apostle states that the Lord was born without father in exactly the same way as he was without mother; if you understand how he was without father, you can understand how he is without mother. If you cannot believe he was without father, in the same way he cannot be understood as without mother. But why did you not quote the text you found from the Apostle entire and unabridged? You set down part, and concealed part; in order to make a false assertion you took away the words of truth. I can see who was your teacher! You must have been taught by the one whose example you follow. When the devil tempted God in the Gospels, he said. 'If thou be the Son of God, cast thyself from hence. For it is written that: He hath given his angels charge over thee, that they keep thee in all thy ways' (Luke 4:9–10; cf. Psalm 90/91:11). In quoting this, he covered up the words that followed and were close connected, namely, 'Thou shalt walk upon the asp and the basilisk: and thou shalt trample underfoot the lion and the dragon' (Psalm 90/91:13). In his cunning he quoted the previous verse but suppressed the following one; he quoted one to suit himself, he kept silent over the other lest he be himself condemned. He knew well enough that he was the one the prophecy called asp and basilisk, lion and dragon. In the same way you quoted part and suppressed part, citing the words that suit your case, suppressing the others because if you had quoted them all, you would have refuted your own argument.

But it is high time to move on to our final point: we have delayed too long over particular topics, trying to give an ample answer, and have exceeded the bounds of a book which is already too long.

XVII. In another of your treatises, your blasphemies rather, you say, 'He separated the Spirit from the divine nature, he who created his humanity. That which is born of Mary is of the Holy Spirit, who filled with justice that which was created. For it says he was "manifested in the flesh, justified in the spirit" (I Timothy 3:16). The same Spirit made him an object of fear to the demons, "if I by the Spirit of God cast out devils" (Matthew 12:28). Of his flesh he made himself a temple; "I saw the Spirit coming down, as a dove; and he remained upon him" (John 1:32). The same Spirit also granted him elevation into heaven, for it says, "giving commandments to the apostles whom he had chosen by the Holy Ghost he was taken up" (Acts 1:2). It was the same Spirit which gave such glory to Christ in the end.' All that is your writing, your blasphemous claim that Christ had nothing of himself. He did not even receive anything from the Word, the Son of God, being as you assert a mere man, but everything he had was a gift of the Holy Spirit. Now if we can show you that everything you refer to the Spirit was actually his own, it remains only for us to prove that he is God, though you want us to think him no more than a man; whereas you say that all he had came from another, we shall show that it was all his own. We can prove this not only by controversies and arguments but by the very word of God, for there can be no evidence about God more compelling than the divine. No one knows God better than his own majesty, no witness for God is more worthy of credit than the witness he bears about himself.

Firstly, you say that it was the Holy Spirit which created his humanity; we could accept this in its obvious sense did we not know that you had put it forward in a disbelieving way. We cannot deny that the flesh of the Lord was conceived by the Holy Spirit, but we do say that the Spirit co-operated in the conception of the body in such a way that the humanity was created for himself by the Son of God, as the Holy Spirit himself says in the scriptures, in the words, 'Wisdom hath built herself a house' (Proverbs 9:1). See there: what was conceived by the Holy Spirit was built and perfected by the Son of God. Not that the work of the Son of God was something other than the work of the Holy Spirit, but because of the union of divinity and majesty, the work the Spirit did was the formation of the Son of God, the formation of the Son of God was by the co-operation of the Holy Spirit. Therefore we read not only that the Holy Spirit came upon the Virgin, but also that the power of the Most High overshadowed her. Since Wisdom is the fullness of divinity, no one should doubt that the whole fullness of divinity existed in that Wisdom who built herself a house. How wretched, how foolish the blasphemy which strives to separate Christ from the Son of God, and does not see that the nature of Divinity is renewed in itself! Are we to believe that the house was built by the Holy Spirit because he was unfitted and unable to build his own house? It is ridiculous and insane to imagine that he who created everything in heaven and on earth by his command was unable to construct himself a body. Especially since the power of the Holy Spirit was his own power, and the divinity and majesty of the Trinity are so united and inseparable that nothing that we can understand about one person of the Godhead is able to be separated from the divinity as a whole. Now if we understand what we are saying, on the evidence of Holy Scripture, that the Holy Spirit came upon Mary and the power of the Most High overshadowed her, and Wisdom built herself a house, the rest of your blasphemous slander is reduced to nothing. There can be no doubt that he made all things, of himself and in himself, and through faith in his name nothing is impossible to those who trust in him. He needed no outside help, neither do those who trust in his power need any such additional help. Therefore all your assertions are futile and sacrilegious, when you say that he was justified by the Spirit, that the Spirit made him an object of dread to the demons, that his flesh was formed by the Spirit into a temple, that it was by the Spirit that he was taken up into heaven. Not that we should imagine that in all these things which Christ did for himself he was lacking the unity and co-operation of the Spirit, for he was never without the Godhead, and all that our Saviour did was in the power of the Trinity, but you seem to want the Holy Spirit to be at work on Our Lord Jesus Christ as if he himself were poor and weak, granting things to him which he was not able to achieve on his own. Learn, then, to believe God in his holy scriptures, learn not to mix falsehood with truth, for the facts are against you, reason prohibits you from confusing the ideas of the evil spirit with the Word of God.

XVIII. You wanted to cite the witness of the Apostle Paul for your assertion that the Spirit filled its own creation with justice, quoting the text, 'he was manifested in the flesh, justified by the Spirit' (I Timothy 3:16). But both your points are insane, your argument irrational. In wanting him to have been filled with justice by the Spirit, you are making him out to have been empty, when you assert that the fullness of justice was granted him. In using the text of St Paul like this, you are depriving the Word of God of both context and sense. The Apostle did not write it in the curtailed and selective way you have quoted it. What did he say? 'And evidently great is the mystery of godliness, which was manifested in the flesh, was justified in the spirit.' Do you see? It was the 'mystery (or sacrament) of godliness' which St Paul says was justified. He could not be so inconsistent with his own writings, his own teaching, as to say he was wanting in justice, for he had always called him 'justice', as in, 'who is made unto us [wisdom and] justice and sanctification and redemption' (I Corinthians 1:30). Also, 'but you are washed; but you are sanctified; but you are justified in the name of our Lord Jesus Christ' (I Corinthians 6:11). How far from him it is, then, to need any fullness of justice, he who filled the whole world with his justice; how false to say his majesty was without justice, when it was his name that justified all things! Can you not see how vain and inept is your blasphemous attempt to deprive Our Lord of that justice, which is ever poured out in abundance by him upon all his faithful, and is never diminished in him despite his lavish giving?

XIX. Next you claim that it was the Spirit that made him an object of fear to the demons. The very absurdity of the claim makes us reject it, and refutes it, but we will still give you some proofs. Tell me, therefore, if as you say the fact that the demons feared him was not his own attribute but another's, not the power within him, but something he had received; how is it that his very name had that power which you say he himself had not? How were demons cast out in his name, the sick cured, the dead raised? The Apostle Peter said to the lame man who sat at the beautiful gate of the Temple, 'In the name of Jesus Christ, arise and walk' (Acts 3:6). Later, in the city of Joppa, he said to the man who had lain paralysed on his bed for eight years, 'Eneas, the Lord Jesus Christ healeth thee; arise and make thy bed' (Acts 9:34). St Paul likewise said to the divining spirit, 'I command thee, in the name of Jesus Christ, to go from her' (Acts 16:18). And the demon went out.

You can see how far from the truth it is that the Lord was powerless when I point out how far from powerless were those whom he made strong by his name. We can read how there was no weakness, from the devil or elsewhere, that could restrict any of the apostles, after the Lord's resurrection. So how did the Spirit need to make him an object of fear when he himself granted that characteristic to others? How could he be weak in himself, when even for others faith in him gained dominion over all things? In addition, those who received power from God never used that power as if it were their own, but referred the power back to him from whom they had received it. The power never had any effect on its own except through the name of him who gave it. Therefore the apostles, like all the servants of God, did nothing in their own name, but only by the invocation of the name of Christ; their power received its effect only from the one who was its source. Did it not stem from its originator, it could not operate through his servants. But you claim that the Lord was just like one of his servants, since as the apostles had nothing of their own except what they received from the Lord, so you want the Lord himself to have had nothing except what he received from the Spirit. Thus you imagine that what he did have he did not possess as Lord but received as a servant. So tell me, how did he use that power? As his own, or as something received? What do we read about him? 'Arise,' he said to the paralytic, 'take up thy bed and go into thy house' (Matthew 9:6). To the father who pleaded for his son, he said, 'Go thy way. Thy son liveth' (John 4:50). When the only son of his mother was being carried to his grave, he said, 'Young man, I say to thee, arise' (Luke 7:14). Did he ever ask for power to be given him for his work, by the invocation of the divine name, as is done by those who have received power from God? As the apostles worked through his name, why did not he work through the name of the Spirit? What are we told about his very preaching? 'For he was teaching them as one having power; and not as their scribes and Pharisees' (Matthew 7:29). Are you going to assert that he was proud or arrogant, in claiming as his own the power which according to you he had received from God? How do we face the fact that power never operates in servants unless they invoke the name of its originator, and it is never of any effect if they use it to make any claims for themselves?

XX. Is that clear enough? Do we need any further argument against your insane blasphemy? We have heard God himself speak to his disciples, 'Heal the sick, raise the dead, cleanse the lepers, cast out devils' (Matthew 10:8). And again, 'In my name you shall cast out devils' (Mark 16:17). Could he have needed the name of another in order to exercise his power, when he made his own name a name of power? What more does he say? 'Behold, I have given you power to tread upon serpents and scorpions and upon all the power of the enemy' (Luke 10:19). He said of himself, and truly, that he was 'meek and humble of heart' (Matthew 11:29), so how could he have told them to work in his name, using his supreme power, if he himself operated in the name of another? Could he have given something to others, as if it were his own, if it is true what you say that he did not possess it but received it from another? Is that how any of the saints worked, those who did receive their power from God? Would not St Peter have been thought insane, St John raving, St Paul demented, if they had spoken thus to the sick: 'In our name, arise'? To the lame, 'In our name, walk'? To the dead, 'In our name, live'? To anyone at all, 'We give you power to tread upon serpents and scorpions and upon all the power of the enemy'? Can you not see from this how absurd you are? If such words would be absurd when spoken out of human presumption, you are all the more absurd in not understanding that they refer to the power of God. You must admit one or the other: either a man can possess divine power, and be able to give it, or if no man could do so, then it must have been God who did. No one could confer divine power as a gift, unless he possessed it by his own nature.

XXI. The next point you made, in your blasphemy, as that it was the Spirit who made his flesh a temple, because John the Baptist said, 'I saw the Spirit coming down from heaven; and he remained upon him' (John 1:32). You attempt to support your mad ideas by the Word of God; so let us see whether the text you have quoted will bear the meaning you claim. 'I saw the Spirit coming down, as a dove; and he remained upon him.' Tell me, if you can, which is the more powerful, the greater, the more honourable? Was it the one who descended, or the one upon whom he descended? The one who conferred honour, or the one upon whom honour was conferred? Where does your text say that the Spirit made his flesh a temple? How did it diminish the honour of God, if God himself descended, to manifest God to the human race? We cannot think that the one whose dignity was proclaimed was any less than the one who did the proclamation. There can be no such distinction made within the divinity, for Godhead is one, and each Person is equal in power; any wicked idea of inequality is totally excluded. In the case in question the person of the Father was present, as was that of the Son and that of the Holy Spirit: it was God the Holy Spirit who descended, God the Son on whom he descended, God the Father who gave witness. None of them had greater honour, none was wronged in any way, but all things related to the whole Godhead, for the honour of any one person of the Trinity redounds to the glory of the whole. There is no need to say more about this, unless it be to demonstrate the original source of your impiety. When thorns and brambles spring up from their roots they make it clear what sort of plant they are; from their appearance they reveal their species. In the same way you are the thorny sprout from the Pelagian heresy, revealing in your growth what your father Pelagius is supposed to have been at the root. Leporius, who claimed to be the disciple of Pelagius, said that Our Lord became the Christ at his baptism: you say that in his baptism he was made the temple of God by the Spirit. The words you say are not the same, but the ideas are equally perverse.

XXII. After the absurdities we have already quoted, your next point is that it was the Spirit who granted the Lord's ascension into heaven. This shows how wicked your opinions are, as if Our Lord Jesus Christ were so weak and ineffective that unless the Spirit were to raise him up to heaven, he would have had to remain on the earth to the present day. You quote the Word of God to make your case, saying that 'giving commandment to the apostles whom he had chosen, by the Holy Ghost he was taken up' (Acts 1:2). Now what am I to make of you, what can I call you? By distorting the Word of God, you have made the sacred text lose its value as evidence. This is a novel form of audacity, trying to make the truth confirm a falsehood with wicked ingenuity. Because what you quote is not what the Acts of the Apostles says. What is it really? 'All things which Jesus began to do and teach, unto the day on which, giving commandment to the apostles whom he had chosen by the Holy Ghost, he was taken up.' To paraphrase it, we should understand, 'the things which Jesus began to do and teach, unto the day on which he was taken up, giving commandment to the apostles whom he had chosen by the Holy Ghost.' There is no need to give you a fuller reply than you really deserve on account of that text, for it would be enough to quote the integral text to demonstrate the whole truth, if you could establish a falsehood simply by corrupting it. But if you believe Our Lord Jesus Christ was not capable of ascending into heaven without being taken up by the Spirit, tell me how he could say, 'No man hath ascended into heaven, but he that descended from heaven, the Son of Man who is in heaven' (John 3:13). You must agree that it is absurd and foolish to say he was incapable of ascending into heaven, when he says he was never absent from heaven though he had descended to the earth. Was he not able to leave the depths and ascend into heaven, though even while he dwelt on earth he was able still to remain in heaven? What about these further words of his, 'I ascend to my Father' (John 20:17)? In this ascension, did he indicate that he would need the help of another, when he states the fact that he was about to ascend as a proof of his own ability and power? David himself speaks of the Lord's ascension, 'God is ascended with jubilee: and the Lord with the sound of the trumpet' (Psalm 46/7:6). He shows us the glory of the one who ascended through his very ability to ascend.

XXIII. So now let us look at the final addition to your blasphemy. You claim that it was the Spirit 'who gave glory to Christ'. You call it glory, you turn it into an insult! For in saying that Our Lord needed to be given glory, you are blaspheming that he was in need of it, since you say he received it. That is what your wicked opinion leads to: in showing how generous was the giver, you demonstrate how poor the receiver was. What a miserably perverse idea! Where do we find the Word of God itself prophesying about Our Lord Jesus Christ, as he ascended into heaven? 'Lift up your gates, O ye princes, and the King of Glory shall enter in.' And he replies to himself with a question, as Holy Scripture often does, 'Who is this King of Glory?' adding at once, 'The Lord who is strong and mighty: the Lord mighty in battle.' Under the image of a battle, he shows how the Lord is victorious in his triumph. Then to complete the matter, he repeats the previous verse, demonstrating by his conclusion how majestic is the Lord as he enters heaven, with the words, 'The Lord of hosts, he is the King of Glory' (Psalm 23/4:7–10). Lest we should think the human body he took on diminished his sublime divinity, he teaches us here that the Lord of hosts is the same as the King of heavenly Glory, he whom he had earlier proclaimed as conqueror in the battle against hell. Now see if you can claim that the Lord's glory was given to him, when the prophecy has told us he is the King of Glory! He says as much about himself: 'when the Son of Man shall come in his glory' (Matthew 25:31). Find some way to contradict that, if you can! He himself bears witness that he possesses his own glory, and you are asserting that he received it from another. We tell you that he had his own proper glory, though that is not to deny that the same property of glory is common to him with the Spirit and the Father. For whatever property there is of God, is of the whole Godhead; the Kingdom of Glory is proper to the Son of God, but it is not therefore isolated from the property of the whole Godhead.

XXIV. Now it really is time to finish this book, or rather my whole work. But I would like to add some quotations from holy men and distinguished bishops, so that we can confirm by modern writings what we have already proved on the authority of Holy Scripture.

Saint Hilary was a man distinguished for every virtue, his writings are as eloquent as his life. He was a bishop, the ruler of a church, and achieved greatness not through his own merits alone but also through the benefits he conferred on others. During the storms of persecution he stood unmoved, and won the status of a confessor by the strength of his undaunted faith. In his first book on the faith (*De Trinitate* Book I) he testifies that Our Lord Jesus Christ is true God from true God, born before the ages, and afterwards begotten as man. In the second book, 'The one only-begotten God grew within the Virgin's womb in the form of a human embryo; he who contains all things, and in whom are all things, was brought forth in the manner of human childbirth' (Book II, 25). In the same book, 'The Angel gave witness that God is with us, he who is born' (II, 27). In the tenth book, 'We teach that the mystery of God was born as man, brought forth by the Virgin.' In the same book, 'For when God was born as man, his birth was not such that he ceased to be God' (X, 7). The same author writes, in the preface to his Commentary on St Matthew's Gospel, 'It was first of all necessary for us that the Only-begotten God, should for our sake be recognized as God, which he was, and born as man, which he had not been before.' In the same place, 'A third conclusion follows, that God be born as man in the world ...' (from a lost work).

These are just a few quotations out of many. They are enough for you to be able to see that St Hilary clearly and publicly preached that God was born of Mary. Where does he echo your idea that 'a creature cannot bring forth the Creator, and what is born of flesh is flesh'?

It would take too long to give an adequate account of each author, so we shall list them rather than analyse what they said. Their own writings are sufficient for you to work on.

XXV. St Ambrose was a famous bishop of God, who never left the Lord's hand, but shone like a jewel on the finger of God. In the book addressed to the Virgins, he tells us, ' "My brother is white and ruddy (Canticles 5:10)"; white, for he is the splendour of the Father; ruddy because he was born of the Virgin. Remember that the glory of his divinity predated the mystery of his body. He did not begin to be of the Virgin, but he who existed came into the Virgin' (*Ad virgines* I, 46). The same writer, in his sermon on the Lord's Nativity, says, 'See the wonder of the Mother of the Lord: a virgin conceived, a virgin gave birth; she was a virgin in giving birth, a virgin in pregnancy, a virgin after giving birth. As is said by Ezechiel, "This gate was shut. It was not opened, because the Lord hath entered in by it (Ezechiel 44:2)." How glorious her virginity, how splendid her fruitfulness! The Lord of the world is born, and there was no groan in childbirth; the womb was emptied and a real child emerged, but her virginity was not broken. It was right that the birth of God should bring a new merit to chastity; his birth did not sully what was intact, for he came to restore what had been sullied' (from a lost text). Again, in his commentary on St Luke's Gospel, he writes, 'She in particular was chosen to give birth to God, she who had been betrothed to a man' (*Comm. on Luke*, II, 1). He clearly preaches that God was born of the Virgin, he names Mary as the Mother of God. What room is there for your vile and unprecedented complaint, 'How can she be the mother of one whose nature is other than hers? If she is called mother by them, it is the humanity that was born, not the Godhead.' But look: that distinguished teacher of the faith says she who gave birth was human, the one who was born was God. This is not a reason for disbelief, but the wonder of our faith.

XXVI. Saint Jerome, the instructor of all Catholics, whose writings shine on the whole world like the lamps of God, writes in his book for Eustochium, 'The Son of God was made the Son of Man for our salvation: he waited ten months in the womb to be born; he whose grasp encloses the world was contained within a narrow cradle' (Epistle 22, 39). In his commentary on Isaiah, he writes, 'The Lord of hosts, who is the King of Glory, descended into the virgin's womb; he went in and came out through the eastern gate which is ever closed (Ezechiel 44:2). Of him Gabriel said to the Virgin, "The Holy Ghost shall come upon thee and the power of the Most High shall overshadow thee. And therefore also the Holy which shall be born of thee shall be called the Son of God" (Luke 1:35) And in Proverbs, "Wisdom hath built herself a house."' (Proverbs 9:1; *Comm. in Isaiam*, III, c. 7, 14). Compare that with your teaching, if you please, with your blasphemies. You say, 'God is the creator of the months, he was not by months brought forth.' Look, Jerome is a man of surpassing learning, approved and sound in his teaching. In almost the very words with which you deny that the Son of God was by months brought forth, he informs us that he was brought forth after months. 'He waited ten months in the womb to be born,' says Jerome: but maybe you think he is a man of little authority. But remember that everybody should use the same turn of phrase, for anyone who does not deny that the Son of God was born of the Virgin, will admit that he was by months brought forth.

XXVII. Then there is Rufinus, a student of Christian philosophy, and no inconsiderable partner of the teachers of the Church. He tells us, in his explanation of the Creed, about the Lord's nativity, 'The Son of God is born of the Virgin, not related to us in the flesh alone, but in his soul which is the link between the Godhead and the flesh; so he was begotten' (*On the Creed*, cap. 13). Is that too obscure a reference to God being born of man? Take Augustine, the great bishop of Hippo Regius: he says, 'As men are born of God, first of all God is born of man, for Christ is God. Christ, born of men, sought only a mother on earth, for he had a Father already in heaven. He was born of God, by whom we were made; he was born of woman, through whom we are remade.' And elsewhere, 'The Word was made flesh, and dwelt among us. Why be surprised, for men are born of God. See, God himself was born of man' (*In evang. Ioh.* II, 15). Again, in his letter to Volusianus, 'Moses and the other prophets prophesied truly about Our Lord the Christ, and gave him great glory. They foretold that he would come, not as their equal, not as their superior in the same sort of miraculous ability, but plainly as Lord and God of all, made man for the sake of men. He therefore willed to do these things, for it would be absurd if he were not himself to do what he had done through others. Beyond that, he had to do some things proper to himself: namely to be born of a Virgin, to rise from the dead and to ascend into heaven. If you think that is not enough to show he is God, I know not what more you can ask' (Epistle 137, 4).

XXVIII. Perhaps you imagine that the authors we have mentioned are of little authority, because they live in distant regions of the world? That would be absurd, because the Faith does not change with travel, and we should estimate someone by who, not where, they are. Our faith unites us all, and those who are agreed in belief can be recognized as forming a single body. Nevertheless I will give you some examples from the East, which you will surely not despise.

St Gregory (Nazianzen) was a brilliant spark of wisdom and erudition: although he is now dead, he lives still in his authoritative teaching; his physical presence is withdrawn from the churches, but his words and his authority remain. He tells us, 'When God came forth from the Virgin, in the human nature which he had assumed, he formed a unity from two natures that had been opposed to each other, the flesh and the spirit; one was assumed into the Godhead, the other is manifest in the grace of divinity. How strange, how unexpected this union! What a wonderful and sublime conjunction! He who was, becomes; he who creates is created. He who is immeasurable, is confined, with the soul as the medium between God and the flesh. He who makes all rich, becomes himself poor' (*Oration* XXXVIII, on the Saviour's Birth). Speaking of the Epiphany, he says, 'What is happening among us, or for us? A new and unheard-of combination of natures has come to be; God has become man.' Again, 'And the Son of God began to be also the Son of Man; not changed from what he was, for he is unchangeable, but taking on what he had not. For he is merciful, and he who cannot be contained can contain' (*Oration* XXXIX). Do you see how clearly, and how splendidly, Gregory proclaims the majesty of God, to teach us the dignity of his incarnation? From all this, the admirable doctor of the faith knew what a surpassing benefit God conferred on us as he came into the world, with no diminution of his honour; for all the good that God offers to man should never lessen his dignity, but ever increase our love for him.

XXIX. Then there is Athanasius, the bishop of Alexandria, a model of steadfast virtue. The persecuting storms of heresy could not shake him, but they proved his worth. His life shone like a mirror, and he nearly acquired a martyr's crown, before gaining the dignity of a confessor. Let us see what he thought about Our Lord Jesus Christ, and about the mother of the Lord. 'As we have often said,' he writes, 'the intention and scope of Holy Scripture is that there is a twofold nature in the one Saviour. He was God always, he is the Son, the Word, the Light, the Wisdom of the Father. And afterwards he took flesh for our sake, from the Virgin Mary, the Theotokos, and was made man' (*Contra Arianos* or. IV). Elsewhere he says, 'There were many holy men who were cleansed from sin; Jeremiah was sanctified from the womb, and John the Baptist while in his mother's womb exulted with joy at the voice of Mary, the *Theotokos*.' To repeat his words, I speak the faith of the whole Church: God, the Son of God, is the Word, the Light, the Wisdom of the Father, and for us took flesh; and for that reason Athanasius calls Mary the *Theotokos*, for she is the Mother of God.

XXX. Hear now the words of John (Chrysostom), the flower of bishops of Constantinople, who attained the glory of martyrdom though no barbarian persecution raged; hear what he believed and what he preached about the incarnation of the Son of God: 'He, whom neither heaven nor earth, nor the seas nor any created thing could have contained, had he come in his sheer divinity, was carried in the womb of the immaculate Virgin' (unknown text). He is one whose faith and teaching you ought to accept, even if you ignore the others, for it was in love and affection for him that his pious people chose you to be their bishop. When they called you from the church of Antioch as their prelate, just as they had called him from there before, they believed they would find in you what they had just lost in him.

So did not all these doctors preach as they did in a spirit of prophecy to confound your blasphemies? You declare that Our Lord and Saviour was Christ, but not God: they call him Christ, the Lord, true God. You rave about Mary being *Christotokos*, but not *Theotokos*; they believe she is *Christotokos* indeed, from which they recognize her as *Theotokos*. It is not only the facts that are opposed to your blasphemies, but the words that describe them, so that you cannot fail to see that God had already prepared an unassailable bulwark against your infidelity, so that when the storm of your heretical assault came it might break against the wall of truth they had already prepared. And can you, most impious, most wicked contaminator of the Great City, you pernicious virus spreading among a holy Catholic people, dare you stand up in the Church of God and speak; how dare you defame, in raving blasphemous words, those bishops of incorrupt faith and Catholic profession, as if the people of the City of Constantinople had been taught wrongly by their former leaders? Are you the one to correct those bishops who went before you? Are you to condemn the prelates of old? Are you more excellent than Gregory, more upright than Nectarius, more distinguished than John? Are you greater than all the bishops of the East, who may not have been as famous as those I have named, but did share their faith?

I have said enough to conclude this matter; when we speak about the faith, all must agree with the greatest and the best, for thus they can be in union with those great ones.

XXXI. And so I myself, obscure and lowly as my reputation is, as indeed it deserves to be, I myself cannot claim a place as teacher among the great bishops of Constantinople, but I can presume to claim that I was their pupil, and hold them dear. I was taken up by bishop John, of happy memory, into the sacred ministry, and consecrated to God, so that while absent in body I am with you in affection; even though I cannot be present to mingle with that people, so dear to me, so devoted to God, yet I am united with them in thought. That is why I felt for them and shared their grief, breaking out into cries of pain and sadness with them; that is why I did what little I could, in the tearful complaint of my writings, to protest about their injury as if it were to my own organs and limbs. St Paul tells us, the whole body grieves and suffers together if one small part is in pain, so how much more should a small member sympathise with the pain of the greater part? It would be monstrous if the lesser members failed to share in the suffering of the greater members of the very same body, if the greater ones sympathise with the lesser.

Therefore I beseech you all, you who dwell within the circuit of the walls of Constantinople, you fellow citizens of mine in affection for our home, you my brothers in our united faith; I beseech you to separate yourselves from that Nestorius, that ravening wolf, 'who eats up my people as he eats bread' (Psalm 52/3:5). 'Touch not, taste not' anything of his, 'which all are unto destruction' (Colossians 2:21–2). 'Go ye out from him, be ye separate, touch not the unclean thing' (II Corinthians 6:17). Remember those who taught you, your high priests; remember Gregory who is famous throughout the world; Nectarius, glorious in his holiness; John, who was wonderful in his faith and purity. Remember John, I tell you, that John who was in the true mould of John the evangelist, the disciple of Jesus, the apostle, who reclined ever on the breast of the Lord in his affection. Remember him, imitate him, ponder on his purity, his faith, his teaching, his holiness. Remember him who was always your teacher, your nurse, in whose bosom, within whose embrace you grew up. He was your master, and mine as well, we are all his pupils, his novices. Read what he wrote, hold firm to what he told you, cling to his faith and his works. True, it he would be hard to emulate, but it is fair and sublime to imitate him. In these great matters it is praiseworthy to imitate even though we cannot hope to achieve, for no one will fail totally to share in the glory of that achievement, if they have only attempted to copy it or to aspire to it. Keep John Chrysostom ever in mind, keep him before your eyes, think of him, ponder him. Let him recommend to you even these writings of mine, for it was he who taught me what I have written. Because of that you can believe that these are not my words but his, for a stream belongs to its source, and anything attributed to a disciple ought to be referred entirely to the honour of his master.

And so to you, God, the Father of Our Lord Jesus Christ, beyond all things and above all things, I call with voice and mind at once, beseeching you to pour out the gift of your love on all I have written, out of the fullness of your bounty. He himself has taught us, he, Our Lord and God, your Only-begotten son, that you 'so loved the world, as to give your only-begotten Son, . . . that the world may be saved' (John 3:16–17). Grant therefore that through the Incarnation of your only-begotten Son, these your people whom you have redeemed may know your generosity, and his love. May they all understand, with love, that your only-begotten Son, Our Lord and God, was born for us, suffered and rose again; so that the praise of his glory may proceed from our love. Let not his lowliness cause any to think there was any diminution of his honour, but let it always cause charity to increase. May we all be aware, in devotion and wisdom, of the graces bestowed by your mercy, so that we may know that the debt we owe to our God is as great as the humility which God took upon himself for our sake.

✠

www.ingramcontent.com/pod-product-compliance
Lightning Source LLC
Chambersburg PA
CBHW022025090426
42739CB00006BA/283